The BEST
Shift of Your Life

The BEST
Shift of Your Life

✦

The Restaurant Manager's Guide to Success
Outside the Restaurant!

Kathleen Wood

iUniverse, Inc.
New York   Bloomington

iUniverse books may be ordered through booksellers or by contacting:

iUniverse
1663 Liberty Drive
Bloomington, IN 47403
www.iuniverse.com
1-800-Authors (1-800-288-4677)

ISBN: 978-0-595-52618-5 (sc)
ISBN: 978-0-595-62670-0 (ebook)
ISBN: 978-0-595-51488-5 (dj)

Printed in the United States of America

iUniverse rev. date: 2/05/2010

This book is dedicated to you. May you always have
The BEST Shift of Your Life!

Foreword

Shortly after I met Kathleen Wood in 1994, I had the opportunity to witness the essence of her career and her leadership in a vignette that is still a vivid memory. She was the manager of a young and mostly inexperienced sales and marketing team working for the Educational Foundation of the National Restaurant Association. It was the kickoff of the Restaurant Show—the big event, five days of non-stop activity that is a mental and physical grind for those who work the entire show. The team sold products and services to educate restaurateurs about food safety, a mission that, while valuable, was not necessarily the equivalent of curing cancer or creating the next great tech startup in the garage.

However, you would not have known that watching Kathleen fire up her team for the show. The energy was electric, the standard was platinum, the expectations were to exceed whatever had been accomplished before, and the pace was guaranteed to be fast, unrelenting, and demanding. Her team looked great; they were pros, they took their vitamins, they smiled, and they radiated back the confidence that Kathleen instilled in each and every one of them that they were going to conquer that show. There was no doubt in any of their minds that they were not just selling a product—they were making the industry, and the life of every consumer who would eat in a restaurant, better and safer. She taught, trained, modeled, coached, cajoled, required, and she led step-by-step—in a way that set her team up to succeed. Five minutes into seeing Kathleen in action, I knew she was one of those rare talents who would someday find ways to influence an enormous number of people lucky enough to get swept up in her passions and her path.

Ask a colleague about Kathleen and the words that are quickly used to describe her are smart, dynamic, energetic, creative, tireless, inspirational, generous, amazing, real, talented, and very funny. She is all of that and more, and in *The Best Shift of Your Life* she has drawn from her experiences in life, education, and work to create a blueprint for finding the way to fulfill your dreams, accomplish your goals, and enjoy the fruit of happiness along the way. Just as she led that sales team fifteen years ago, she has written this book in a step-by-step fashion that makes it easy to read and use.

I frequently share stories about how Kathleen helped me from the very beginning to shape the vision for our People Report consortium, and to build it into the resource that it is today for the service sector workforce and the foodservice industry. Her advice, encouragement, and unfailing belief in our work were constants that made the difference on many occasions. This past June, as the closing keynote speaker for our workforce symposium, Kathleen introduced this book to a raptly attentive audience who laughed, cried, took furious notes, and then gave her a standing ovation as she finished. I learned later that day that it was her first standing ovation—I am quite positive it won't be her last. Kathleen has been paying it forward her entire career, and this book is just the next installment. It is a privilege and a pleasure to wish every reader The Best Shift of Your Life!

Joni Thomas Doolin
CEO + Founder, People Report

Contents

Acknowledgments

It took me a long time to learn that none of us succeeds by ourselves. Thankfully, I made a great shift and now ask and allow people to help me. My friend and advisor, Richard Damien, once told me that "writing a book is the universe's way of helping writers seek their own clarity." What has become abundantly clear to me in writing this book is that it has been achieved with a tremendous amount of love and support from so many people.

Thank you—these are two words that seem somewhat inadequate to express my love, gratitude, and appreciation for all of the insights, lessons, and experiences that have been shared with me.

I have to start by thanking the cornerstone of my life—my family— who has been there for me through the entire journey of this book: my loving sisters, Mary Caba and Sue Tierno, who have always been willing participants in my journeys and who have been equally gracious in letting me travel on theirs. We are the "WOTIBA" tribe for life! I would like to thank my brothers-in-law, nieces, and nephews—Mary's family: Kerry, Brian, and Courtney; and Sue's family: Joe, Jen, Joe, Jim, and Julie. They have all been a constant source of joy, happiness, and unconditional love in my life. We have all shared so many amazing and memorable journeys together. My nieces and nephews are exceptional young people who give me great faith in what the future holds. Of course, my parents, Jean and Ed Wood—though they are no longer here—are always in my heart. I know they are smiling down and are proud of their life's legacy.

I would like to thank my board of directors, friends, and mentors who have all contributed to my journey: Julie Opheim, Catherine Kreston, Erin Davey Jordan, Joni Doolin, Phil Friedman, Todd Graves, Lori Daniel, Valerie Loew, Edna Morris, Kelli Valade, Richard Damien, Wally Doolin, David Goronkin, Matthew Chustz, Loret Carbone, Pat Harris, Julia Stewart, Hala Moddelmog, Carla Cooper, Jamie Griffin, Louise van der Does, Anne Varano, Roz Mallet, Teresa Siriani, Leslie Christon, Margie McCartney,

Randi Kirshbaum, Maryclaire Piccoli, Kevin Hall, Tim McCarthy, Diana Purcell, Christopher O'Donnell, George Macht, Dan Gescheidle, Julie Carruthers, Toni Kottom-Quist, Rodney Morris, Susan Steinbrecher, Tami Kaiser, Harry Bond, Joleen Goronkin, Jon Luther, Tony Santarelli, Steve Pettise, Sally Smith, Greg Theisen, Rick Van Warner, Don FitzGerald, Bernadette Kane, Dave Anderson, Jennifer Percival, Mary O'Connor, Larry Reeher, Gerry White, Sue Wasylik, Cathy Levielle, Lyn Devorkin, Mary Jo Larson, Karen Keown, Alan Gould, Ellen Koteff, Debi Benedetti, Deb Nelms, Sue Elliott, Amanda Hite, Mary Lou Hunter, Joe Micatrotto, Kerry Kramp, Randy Lopez, Melissa Papaleo, Chuck Winship, Rick Silva, Terrian Barnes, Norris Bernstein, Carron Harris, Pokey Chatman, Gerry Fernandez, Tara Davey, Alice Elliot, Linda Pharr, Fritzi Woods, Devin Bonner, Brandy Rush, Celton Hayden, Andy Feinstein, Jennifer Bayer, Christina Marciante, Jennifer Tierney, Carolyn McCormick, Mike Moon, Richard McDonald, Luke Greer, Sid Feltenstein, Carin Stutz, Steve King, Barbara Kane, Kathleen Gilmartin, Marty Weinberg, Damon Hininger, John Ferguson, Eliot Swartz, Carolyn Greely, Ian Vaughn, Ian Herrera, Ken Green, John Drummond, Bill Allen, Rick Federico, Bryce King, Terri Krause, Craig Silvey, Lynn Ruby, Elka Roberts, Catalina Ganis, Joan Ray, Sean Self, Sandy Pritchard, Susan Feniger, and Patty Duffey. And to the countless other special people who have supported me and helped me—please know you will always have a place in my heart.

I would also like to extend a special thank you to all the crew members of Raising Cane's Chicken Fingers, who I had the honor of working with during my tenure with the company. We were brought together by a passion for *One Love*, and we are bonded for life by one hurricane—Hurricane Katrina. Your courage and commitment to rebuild your communities are *huge*.

I have been very fortunate to work with amazing leaders both inside and outside the restaurant industry. I would like to recognize the executives and leaders of companies who have believed in me as much as I have believed in them:

American Express
Baja Fresh
Beef O'Brady's
Border Grill
Brinker International
Buca Inc.
Buffalo Wild Wings
Carlson Hospitality Worldwide
CC's Coffee House

Church's Chicken
Checkers-Rally's
Coca-Cola
Correction Corporation of America
Educational Foundation of the National Restaurant Association
El Pollo Loco
Famous Dave's
Fleming's Prime Steakhouse and Wine Bar
Fuddrucker's
IHOP
MasterCard International
McAlister's Deli
PepsiCo
Perkins and Marie Callendar's
P.F. Chang's
Parco Foods
Taco John's
Two Chefs on a Roll
Village Tavern
Whataburger

In closing, I would like to thank the *thirteen million* men and women in the foodservice and hospitality industry (National Restaurant Association, 2009). Today, this vital industry serves over one billion guests daily and is an essential component in our everyday lives (National Restaurant Association, 2009). I would like to thank all of the leaders, board members, and associations working tirelessly to support this great industry.

Thank you all for a lifetime of support in making my dreams a reality.

The Best Way to Use This Book

- Use this as your guide for creating your best shifts—you can take it as fast or slow as you want.
- Recognize that the book is meant to stretch your thinking, not to stress you out. It will challenge you to examine your life, explore your beliefs, and expand your vision. Be honest with yourself, and don't be afraid of the answers. This book won't force you to change; however, it will likely give you the courage if you do choose to change!
- Don't feel pressured to have all the answers; it is really about exploring the possibilities. Be open, and try the activities before judging whether you can or can't complete them.
- Hopefully you will use this book many times as you go through shifts of life. When you successfully accomplish one shift of life, you will be ready for another, and this book will help you shift to your next level of success.
- It is important to remember that life happens and *shifts* happen! So treat your activities and plan a little like gelatin: solid, yet with room to wiggle.

Lastly, enjoy; this is really for you and about you—there is no judging. The only thing required is your commitment to complete the entire book and to experience the best results possible!

Enjoy and explore *The Best Shifts of Your Life*!

Pre-Shift: Get Fired Up

o o o o o o o o o o o o o o o o o o o o o o o o o o o o o o o o

Find something you're passionate about and keep tremendously interested in it.

—Julia Child, Chef, Author, and Television Personality

Anyone at any time can have the best shift of his or her life. Shifts happen in your life, in your career and in your restaurant. In writing this book, my goal is to take the great lessons from running the best shifts of your restaurant and translate them into running the best shifts of your life. Think about it like this: as a restaurant manager, you have many tools to support you in running great shifts. These include checklists, inventory systems, training guides and operations manuals.

Now, think of another meaning of the word "shift," like "transformation." Shifts in your life can be transformational. These are shifts like defining your career path, identifying your purpose, setting life goals and developing your plan for living a happy and fulfilling life. What tools do you have for managing these kinds of shifts in your life?

I have written this book to support you in leveraging your knowledge of running restaurant shifts to creating the best shifts of your life outside of your restaurant. Its essence reflects my core belief that all shifts have an open, middle, and close, just as a restaurant has an opening shift, a mid shift, and a closing shift. A successful day in a restaurant and a successful shift in your life both require the completion of all three. Just like at a restaurant, sometimes those shifts fly by and sometimes they seem never-ending. The great news is that the more prepared you are for any type of shift, the more success you ultimately achieve!

The book is structured so that it also has an opening, mid and close. The "opening shift" focuses on opening yourself up to your reality. This shift provides you the opportunity to reflect on your life today and to take inventory of where you are relative to where you want to be in your life. The "mid shift" focuses on bridging where you are today to the goals and dreams of your life. The power of the mid shift is the opportunity to visualize your future and develop your own plan of action to realize it. The "closing shift" focuses on sustaining and creating even greater shifts in your life. This is the shift that provides you even more insights and tools for sustaining the amazing shifts of your life.

I have written this book for you, from one manager to another, from one leader to another, and from one passionate restaurant person to another. I wish someone would have given me a practical system like this at any point in my life or career. My hope is that you will use all or part of it to support you in your journey for creating the best shifts of your life.

This book reflects my experiences, my pursuit of knowledge, my passion for the restaurant industry, and my belief in the power of human potential. It also is reflective of my voice, which may not always be grammatically correct, but my focus is more on the message than the punctuation. It is my "give–back" to an industry that has given me so much. It is also my gift for everyone who has ever had the desire to live the life of their dreams and create the best shifts of their lives.

The Shifts of My Life

As you journey through your shifts in this book, I will be sharing experiences from both my life shifts and restaurant shifts. I have always considered myself very fortunate that one of my best life and restaurant shifts was during my first few shifts at John's Pizza, when I absolutely fell in love with the restaurant industry. John's Pizza was a fantastic first job. In a two-year period I went from "phone girl" to bus girl to dishwasher to assistant cook. I was so happy the whole time I was there. I was so excited to be making anywhere from $2.00 an hour to $1.25 per hour plus tips, because I loved the speed, the thrill of the rush, and the joy of celebrating another great shift!

All these years later, I still love the restaurant business. I believe the restaurant industry is one of the greatest businesses in the world. What other industry is there where a person with a little money, a lot of hard work, and a desire to succeed can have the American Dream of owning his or her own business? What other industry can say that two out of five adults, at some point in their careers, have been a part of the industry (National Restaurant Association, 2009)? What other industry is a part of people's lives in both their very best and their most tragic shifts? What other industry has the tremendous capacity to serve the needs of billions around the world? What other industry is such an intrinsic part of so many lives?

When I started out at John's Pizza as a young teenager, did I ever think that decades later I would still have the same love and passion of that young bus girl? Back then, I would have told you that I just loved the action and being part of the "family" of John's Pizza. Today, I am more passionate about the industry than ever before. And being a part of the restaurant industry today is as exciting as when I was just starting out. It truly is an amazing industry.

Over the years, I have made countless speeches for corporations, associations, and colleges and universities, and have facilitated discussion topics related to the foodservice and hospitality industry. I typically start out my sessions by asking the audience questions about the restaurant industry such as the following:

What are the projected annual sales for the restaurant business?

Answer: $566 billion

* Restaurant industry sales on a typical day in 2009: $1.5 billion.
                    (National Restaurant Association's Web site, 2009)

How many restaurants are there in the United States?

Answer: 945,000 restaurants

* One-quarter of eating-and-drinking establishments are owned by women, 15 percent by Asians, 8 percent by Hispanics and 4 percent African-Americans.
* Eating-and-drinking places are mostly small businesses—91percent having fewer than 50 employees.
                    (National Restaurant Association's Web site, 2009)

How many people work in the restaurant industry in the United States?

Answer: 13 million people

* Forty percent of all adults have worked in the restaurant industry at some point during their lives, and more than one out of four adults had their first job experience in a restaurant.
                    (National Restaurant Association's Web site, 2009)

What is the projected economic impact of the restaurant industry in the United States?

- Answer: $1.5 trillion on an annual basis.

  (National Restaurant Association's Web site, 2009)

How many meals are served annually by the restaurant industry in the United States?

Answer: Restaurants will provide more than 70 billion meal-and-snack occasions in 2009.

- On a typical day in America in 2009, more than 130 million people will be foodservice patrons.

  (National Restaurant Association's Web site, 2009)

In how many countries does McDonald's operate?

Answer: McDonald's operates in more than 30,000 local restaurants serving 52 million people in more than 100 countries each day.

- More than 70 percent of McDonald's restaurants worldwide are owned and operated by independent, local men and women.

  (McDonald's Web site, 2009)

When I ask these questions, the answers I get always surprise me, because the numbers are typically so low and so off the mark. The other amazing thing is that people often don't realize the global impact of the foodservice and hospitality industry.

I also ask audiences to share their experiences in the restaurant industry. If they come at it from a customer perspective, they will share either an extremely positive or an extremely negative experience that they have had in a restaurant. If they come at it from an employee perspective, the majority of the time they will share mixed results. The mixed results have always fascinated me because the restaurant industry offers so many opportunities for career advancement. It is definitely an industry in which, if you are willing to work hard, you can achieve great success. It is not an industry that you can "coast" through. There are high expectations and equally high rewards if you choose to be successful in it! I believe that because restaurants employ so many people who are only in it "until they get a real job," there are many people who do not enjoy the industry itself. As a result, it has gained a stigma for being an industry where one cannot have a "true" career.

As I have journeyed through my career, I have also dealt with the "stigma" of the restaurant industry. I have heard it all, from being called a "hamburger flipper" to hearing that it's a last-resort job, it's a vocational-studies job, or it is definitely not something you do for a career. I can remember my high-school guidance counselor telling me that if I kept pursuing this "restaurant stuff," I would end up going nowhere. During my senior year of high school, I was on salary with benefits working in a restaurant, and many of my classmates took pity on me because clearly I was not intelligent enough to have a real job!

I remember graduating from the University of Wisconsin-Stout with my hotel and restaurant degree and everyone thinking I had lost my mind when I made the decision to go into management for a quick-service restaurant company. Many questioned whether that was a great career move. When I applied for graduate school, one of my professors suggested that I drop out because my undergraduate degree was "not a solid platform for the rigors of an MBA." I also recall how proud my family and friends were when I took my first "real" job, working with the newly formed Educational Foundation of the National Restaurant Association. Everyone seemed most excited because I would no longer being wearing a restaurant uniform—even though I had been a successful restaurant operator for over 10 years!

I know that I am not the only one who has heard the "winds of why?" in his or her journey. For me, the "whys" never held me back—I loved what I was doing, and I was thrilled to continue to explore all of the opportunities of the restaurant business. To answer all those who asked "why restaurants?" here are the whys:

I love the fact that being in the restaurant business afforded me the opportunity to work my way through the College of DuPage, the University of Wisconsin-Stout, and, ultimately, my MBA from Loyola University of Chicago.

I love the fact that being in the restaurant industry provided me with the opportunity to be a part of great companies like John's Pizza, McDonald's, Taco Bell, LePeep, Carson Pirie Scott, TGI Friday's, MasterCard International, and Raising Cane's Chicken Fingers.

I love the fact that being in the restaurant industry provided me with the opportunity to be a founder and co-founder of Elliot Solutions, the Elliot Leadership Institute, and Kathleen Wood Partners, LLC.

I love the fact that being in the restaurant industry provides me with the opportunity to be a part of amazing organizations, such as the National Restaurant Association, the Women's Foodservice Forum, the Council of Hotel and Restaurant Trainers, the People Report, the Collins College of Hospitality Management, and the MultiCultural Foodservice and Hospitality Alliance.

I love the fact that being in the restaurant industry provided me, and still provides me, with the opportunity to share my message at industry events across the United States. I love sharing my incredible journey and the lessons I learned along the way with an industry and a generation of managers who are the future of our industry.

I love the fact that being in the restaurant industry has provided me, and still provides me, with multiple lifetimes of experiences, memories, and joy. It is an industry that has been with me during both the best shifts of my life and the absolute worst shifts of my life. I have benefited from having lifelong friends and acquaintances who have supported me in all the shifts of my life.

What I love most about the restaurant industry is that I was just like anyone else when I started my career: I had no family ties or restaurant connections that gave me any special advantages. I was just a young kid who happened to love what I did and who wanted to see, do, and be a part of this incredible industry—and who, in the process, was fortunate enough to enjoy the best shifts of my life.

The future belongs to those who believe in the beauty of their dreams.
—Eleanor Roosevelt

OPENING SHIFT

✦

OPENING SHIFT

The Golden Hour

Bring courage and compassion to all that you do, always have the numbers in your head and the people in your heart. And through it all, be true to yourself.

—Edna Morris, Founder of Women's Foodservice Forum

One of the greatest things about being the opening manager is that one quiet hour before everyone arrives. I call it the "Golden Hour." It is the hour in which the restaurant shines from the night before. You hear only the hum of the hood system. You can still smell last night's special in the air, and you feel the calmness in the kitchen. The Golden Hour is that valuable hour when you can review last night's results, reflect on today's priorities, and prepare and plan for what needs to be done for another successful day.

The Golden Hour is a powerful time to review, reflect, and to reignite your passion for the day. Many managers cherish the Golden Hour of the shift, yet few use the practice of the Golden Hour in life. In today's 24/7 world, your Golden Hour might not be in the morning. It may be at some other point in your day. The key is to find that one Golden Hour each day to reflect upon where you are, where you want to go, and how you will achieve success.

In our very busy lives, we often get so consumed by *doing* that we rarely take time to stop and sit still. Sometimes it is impossible for us to think about sitting still for even a *moment* because our to-do list is so long. We think that any time spent planning takes too much time away from doing, so we try to cram our planning sessions into the five-minute walk from our parking spot to the front door—or worse, while we're on the phone, supposedly listening to our family or friends. As a result, we're in a perpetual state of *doing* and not *planning*. A good restaurant manager would never try to cram the entire preparation for the day into a ten-minute break between lunch and dinner. If you would not do it at work, why would you shortchange your life?

The Golden Hour is a powerful hour. It is a time when you can sit still and reflect on your life, goals, and dreams. In the stillness and calmness powerful thoughts will begin to fill your mind. The secret is that you have most of the answers to your questions. You just need to take the time to listen to yourself! So, take a moment and utilize your Golden Hour to review, reflect, and reignite your passion about *The Best Shift of Your Life*!

Do you remember some of the best shifts of your life? If you're having trouble getting started, don't worry—that's completely normal. The following exercises will get you well on your way to making good use of your Golden Hour. Think back to some of the amazing shifts you have had both in your restaurant and in your life. Try to remember those restaurant and personal shifts where everything went just as you planned. Remember those shifts when you were thrilled by how smoothly and successfully they ran. Now take a moment, and write down what made those the best shifts of your life.

The Best Shift of Your Life—Restaurant

Here are a few thought-starters:

What was one of the best shifts you have had in a restaurant?

What made it a memorable shift?

How did you feel?

How did your team feel?

Were you able to repeat that shift consistently? Why or Why Not?

The Best Shift of Your Life—Personal

Here are a few thought-starters:

What was one of the best shifts you have had in your life? For example, a goal you have achieved, a success in your life, a memorable time or an amazing experience.

What made it a memorable shift?

How did you feel?

How did your family/friends feel?

Were you able to repeat shifts like this consistently? Why or Why Not?

Would you like to learn more about creating the best shifts of your life?

One Dream Activity

As you start to reflect on your best shifts, here is an activity to connect you with your best shifts in both your restaurant and your life. In the next ten minutes, write down one dream and commit yourself to achieving it. The most successful people in the world write down their dreams and goals. This is because even the most organized and successful people can lose sight of a dream or goal that isn't constantly in front of them. By writing it down, you're forbidding yourself to simply forget about it or act as if it never existed. It serves as a reminder of why you're doing what you do each day. Start a new shift now!

If you have never thought of a dream or goal or if it has been awhile, take a moment and think about something you've always wanted to see, do, or be, but thought it was impossible to achieve. These types of big goals and dreams are the first step towards igniting some of the best shifts of your life. Your dream or goal serves as a shining star on good days, bad days, and all of the days in between. You might want to use it as a constant reminder as you read, participate, and journey through this entire book.

Walt Disney once said, "If you see it, then you can believe it and ultimately achieve it."

In the box below, write about one dream or goal you really want to achieve. Please be as specific as possible.

Using your "One Dream" response, answer the following questions.

1. How will your life change when you achieve your dream?

2. How will your relationships change when you achieve your dream?

3. How will you change when you achieve your dream?

4. Describe how you will feel after you achieve your dream.

The power of the Golden Hour is it provides you with the ability to see where you are and where you want to go to make the best shift of your life. It's time to live a life powered by your dreams and goals and to make them your reality!

Nothing will work unless you do.

—Maya Angelou

Opening Checklist:
Love, Like, and Dislike Checklist

Accountability is the thing. If you don't make people accountable for the job they're doing, they're not going to do it.

**—Leah Chase, Co-owner and chef of
New Orleans' landmark restaurant Dooky Chase**

The opening checklist is an essential tool used by successful managers. It serves as a guide to begin the day on track and to move it in the right direction. The opening checklist, when used effectively, ensures that all of the necessary details of opening a restaurant have successfully been addressed. The opening checklist also provides managers with a systematized routine for setting themselves and their shifts up for success.

Sometimes, as managers become more and more familiar with their routine, they stop using the opening checklist. Managers may claim that they no longer need the checklist because they "know what needs to be done." Does the restaurant still open? Typically, yes. However, when the checklist is not used, little things are inevitably overlooked. In the early morning hours, the "little things," such as not checking par levels, doing line checks, or taking the opening inventory, may go unnoticed. As the shift moves into the heat of rush, it is amazing how the "little things" become much more noticeable. Soon, *everyone* feels the pain of the missed items on the checklist!

What is the result of the "little things" building up? The shift becomes increasingly challenging. The shift loses its focus because now everyone is trying to overcome the shortfalls and the shift actually *tanks*. Usually, the only way to recover from a shift that is swiftly moving south is to slow the entire restaurant down and address the issues. Once the issues have been addressed, the shift can pick up speed and begin to move back on track.

Believe it or not, the same thing happens to you in life. You can become so busy with everything until there is a buildup of "little things"—and suddenly, you start thinking: *What is happening to my life? How the heck did I get here? When did everything start heading in this direction?* You realize the impact of all of those "little things" you missed by not using the checklist of your life. In other words, it's time to check in!

Your Reality Check

How do you perceive your life's reality today? Where are you in terms of reaching your goals? How happy are you in your relationships? How connected are you in your community? Do you find your career fulfilling? These are just a few questions to consider when evaluating the reality of your life. There are a lot of people who choose not to look at their reality. One of the greatest gifts you can give yourself in the course of the many shifts of your life is to check your reality. Successful people are always in a constant state of assessing where they are, relative to where they *want* to be. They are very attuned to whether they are on or off course. Knowing where you are and proactively managing your reality is a powerful secret of successful people. Successful people are in control of their destiny *because they are in control of their reality!*

However, the most difficult—and yet, the most *important*—time to look at your reality is when you are challenged, you are struggling, or you feel that you are just not firing on all cylinders.

In *Good to Great*, author Jim Collins describes the Stockdale Paradox. He tells the story of Admiral James Stockdale, who spent eight years as a prisoner of war in Vietnam. Stockdale's coping strategy during those brutal years enabled him to survive, despite the dire circumstances. Stockdale relates that he never lost faith in "the end of the story." As he states: "I never doubted not only that I would get out, but also that I would prevail in the end and turn the experience into the defining event of my life, which in retrospect I would not trade" (Jim Collins, 2001).

When asked who did not survive, Stockdale replied, "The optimists. Oh, they were the ones who said, 'We're going to be out by Christmas.' And Christmas would come and Christmas would go. Then they would say

Easter ... and then Thanksgiving ... and then it would be Christmas again. And they died of a broken heart." (Jim Collins, 2001).

About Stockdale and his remarkable ability to survive, Collins writes, "You must never confuse faith that you will prevail in the end—which you can never afford to lose—with the discipline to confront the most brutal facts of your current reality, whatever they might be" (Jim Collins, 2001). The Stockdale Paradox is an excellent example of facing the honest facts of your reality and then moving forward so that you can attain clarity about your life.

Must you be a prisoner of war before you face your reality? Of course not—but you can be a prisoner of your own perceptions. I have been a prisoner of *my* own perceptions many times. At one point early in my career, I appeared to have it all: I traveled frequently, I had designer clothes, I had money, I was featured frequently in major trade magazines, and I collaborated with CEOs and executives of Fortune 500 companies. I was on top of my game. Though I loved my career, the reality was that I lived my life in a constant state of busyness. I was so busy I was missing the important things in life and I was moving too fast to notice! My life's checklist went out the door, I was no longer living my life by *choice,* I was living it by the pure *adrenaline* rush of being busy.

When I finally slowed down, I saw my reality—my honest reality. The choices I made for my career seemed right, yet the choices I made for the rest of my life were in need of serious revision. I needed several Golden Hours of personal reflection time.

In that reflection I realized:

- My personal life was suffering. The best night to reach me was on Saturday, at home, because my only plan was to catch up on my sleep. My choices had taken me to a place where there was no time for meaningful relationships. Try limiting your friends to people you can meet up with at the airport, and you'll see how quickly this erodes your social life!

- I missed my family and friends, and they missed me! I wanted to see them, yet it never seemed like I had enough time to do it.

- My health took a backseat. My constant travel schedule, late night dinners, and early morning meetings were taking a toll on my ability to exercise, eat well, and sleep. I realized it had been *years* since I had taken a vacation without my cell phone.

How did I get to this reality? There was no one "big thing;" it was the culmination of many "little things" that happened over time. It was the result of not checking my reality, moving fast, and making a lot of quick decisions that ended up creating incremental changes in my life. Over time, these little changes added up to a reality miles away from where I wanted to be regarding certain aspects of life. I had to face my "brutal" facts, no matter how painful, confusing or frustrating it would be.

I did know this: I was the one who had gotten myself there, and I was equally confident that I could get myself out of there, too. As I considered my future, it was clear that the path I was on supported my career lifestyle, but it did not support my *life*.

When I reflected on my adrenaline-filled life there were several decisions I probably would have made differently. That is the brilliance of looking back at your decisions. The key is to learn from your decisions and move forward. I can also say that some of my most important life lessons came from those same decisions I made, and later helped me support others who were going through very similar experiences.

Will I find myself in the whirlwind of the adrenaline again? There is always that possibility. However, checking my reality on a routine basis allows me to consciously make course corrections. So it is important to force yourself to slow down and check your reality, especially when things speed up. It is an incredible phenomenon—see what happens when you slow down and take the time to reflect! Every time I slow down I see the shift that I need to make. It's like how tanking a lunch shift forces a manager to take a step back and see how important the "little things" are to the success of a great shift. The first step in slowing down is to check your reality with the *Love, Like, and Dislike Checklist.*

Life's Love, Like, and Dislike Checklist

I developed the *Love, Like, and Dislike Checklist* to help me assess what I loved, liked, and disliked in my life. It is a great tool for me to consistently check in on my own reality. It helps me keep track of the little things before they become big things. Over time, I saw the power of the *Love, Like, and Dislike Checklist* when I coached both individuals and executives as they created shifts in their lives. It is an invaluable starting place to see clearly the reality of your choices and make sure that you're heading in the direction of your dreams and goals.

I first developed this tool when I was on a cross-country flight. I just started assessing my life, using a checklist of everything I loved, liked, and disliked. By the time I landed, I had a much clearer picture of my reality.

Today, I still regularly use this *Love, Like, and Dislike Checklist* to ensure that I am staying on my life's course.

The objective of the *Love, Like, and Dislike Checklist* is for you to open up and become clearer about your reality today. This is a *snapshot* of where your life is today. The benefit of the *Love, Like, and Dislike Checklist* is that, just like any checklist in the restaurant, you can use it daily, weekly, monthly, quarterly, or annually. It will be especially helpful when you want to make a change, a big decision, or a shift in your life.

Take a few moments to complete the following *Love, Like, and Dislike Checklist*. The best way to complete it is to simply place a check in the column that applies to your current reality. Use the "notes" section to capture your thoughts or jot down reminders to check back on, just like when you complete a checklist in your restaurant. The more you put into this the more you will get out of it. The more accurate your responses, the clearer and more powerful your results will be. You don't want to exaggerate your feelings, of course, but holding back won't help you clarify your reality. This is a great opportunity for you to reflect on the choices you've made and to gain clarity about the choices you *will* make as you go forward in the best shifts of your life!

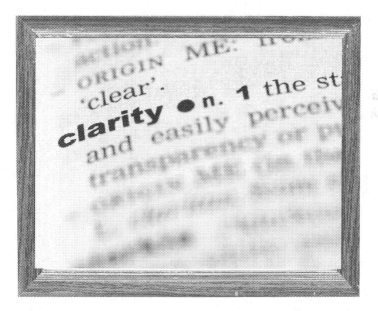

Love, Like, and Dislike Checklist

	Love	Like	Dislike	Notes
Personal—YOU!				
Your life overall				
Balance–work/life				
Life stability				
Energy level				
Your Feelings				
Happiness				
Level of frustration				
Anxiety				
Contentment				
Peace				
Emotional				
Your Health				
Physical health				
Wellness				
Physical fitness				
Exercise habits				
Weight				
Diet				
Sleep habits				
Your Fun				
Hobbies				
Travel				
Vacation				
Sports				
Reading				
Dining				
Movies/theater				
School				
New activities				

Love, Like, and Dislike Checklist

	Love	Like	Dislike	Notes
Your Home				
Location				
Rent/Own				
Roommate				
Décor				
Safety				
Noise				
Your Personal Connections/ Closest Relationship				
Your spouse				
Your significant other				
Other important relationships				
Family				
Your relationships with the following: Parents				
Grandparents				
Children				
Siblings				
Other relatives				
Friends				
Best friends				
Close friends				
Social friends				
Acquaintances				
Lost-touch friends				
Pets				
Number				
Ability to take care of them				
Health				

Love, Like, and Dislike Checklist

	Love	Like	Dislike	Notes
Wealth Creation				
Your career				
Your current job				
Your boss/supervisor				
Your current company				
Your compensation				
Your benefits				
Your future growth opportunities				
Your co-workers				
Your commute				
Your travel				
Business Networks				
Associations (local)				
Volunteering				
Seminars				
Conferences				
Financial Health				
Income				
Savings				
Investment				
Credit card balances				
Debt level				
Loans				
Mortgages				
Financial freedom				
Community Connections				
Community involvement				
Association involvement				
Affiliation involvement				
Volunteer work				
Spirituality				
Place of worship				
Connection to like-minded people				
Connection to your spiritual beliefs and practices				

Love, Like, and Dislike Checklist

Anything Else in Your Life	Love	Like	Dislike	Notes

Love, Like, and Dislike Checklist

Look at your checklist and answer the following questions:

- What am I proudest of?
- What do I feel most successful in?
- What am I happiest about?
- What am I most amazed about?
- What shocks me the most?
- What would I do differently to positively impact my results?
- What would I keep the same?

Complete the following statement by choosing the letter of the response that best describes how you feel about your results.

Overall, _____

- A. I am thrilled with my results. I am ecstatically living the best shifts of my life!
- B. I feel good. I see many positives, but also some opportunities. I am living some pretty good shifts.
- C. I am shocked. I cannot believe this is true—something must be wrong with this form!

Congratulations on completing your first step in gaining greater clarity about your reality—and the choices *you have made in creating it!* No matter what your answers were, you now have some key information to move you forward on your path to creating powerful shifts. The true power of the *Love, Like, and Dislike Checklist* is that it allows you to see patterns in your life. It also lets you see opportunities as you move forward.

The first time I did the *Love, Like, and Dislike Checklist*, I clearly saw that there were many things that I *liked* about my life. But I also clearly saw that many things were missing in my life; I did not have a lot of checks on the left side, the *love* column. I was also amazed at what I checked in the *dislike* column. I looked at the dislike column three times before it hit me; I just did not like certain aspects of my job.

I thought I loved my job but when I looked at the Love, Like and Dislike Checklist closely, I saw that I definitely had an opportunity to improve aspects of my job if I was going to move forward in it. *It was definitely my reality: I really didn't like what was happening in my job.*

Questions flooded my mind. How could I not have noticed? What else had I missed? Did this kind of thing happen to other people, or just me? And, most importantly, *why* did I miss it? It certainly had not happened overnight. It was undeniably a direct reflection of all of these "little" things I had not been paying attention to for awhile.

As I analyzed my *Love, Like, and Dislike Checklist*, I realized that I had a tremendous opportunity to make new choices in my life:

- I had the choice to accept the reality of my *Love, Like, and Dislike Checklist*, or to turn a blind eye to it and hope my reality would improve on its own.
- I had the choice to keep doing the same thing, or I could start making new choices. Essentially, I decided to acknowledge the shortfalls and stop dwelling on them. I threw away any excuses for the reasons that had brought me to that place. I chose to embrace my reality and move forward.
- I had the choice to live with greater awareness and to make this type of checklist a frequent part of my life, just as you have the choice to utilize the opening checklist as a daily habit in your restaurant.

As you assess your *Love, Like, and Dislike Checklist*, you will have choices, too. I encourage you to choose moving forward, toward living your life! Don't whine, wish, or wait for it to happen. Nothing changes that way. You cannot change your past, but you can learn from it. As you complete your *Love, Like, and Dislike Checklist*, accept your past and apply what you have learned to your present so you can move forward to create powerful shifts for your future.

Stepping Back for a Wider Look

As you look at your reality, it is also important to step back and look at the whole picture. I learned that lesson during Hurricane Katrina. At the time, I was in my first two months as the President and COO of Raising Cane's Chicken Fingers, a fast-growing Baton Rouge, Louisiana-based restaurant chain. If Katrina was the nation's largest, greatest natural disaster, our company was one of the greatest recovery stories!

Prior to Hurricane Katrina, there were over three thousand restaurants open in the greater New Orleans area. About a month after Katrina, there were only *thirty* restaurants open—and six of them were Raising Cane's. The crew of Raising Cane's was one of the most amazing groups of people I have ever had the privilege of working with in my career. The tireless effort of every manager and crew member working around the clock to operate restaurants in completely devastated areas of the Gulf Coast was extraordinary. What made it even *more* amazing was the fact that the average age of our employees was between sixteen and twenty-four years old. They were going through their own personal Katrina crises, yet they came to work every day to help their communities return to life.

As leaders, our number-one priority before, during, and after the hurricane was the safety of our crew. We closed our restaurants well in advance of the hurricane so that our crew members and managers could be out of harm's way. We had a comprehensive crisis-management system in place to ensure that we were well prepared, could stay connected during the hurricane, and had backup resources to support our crew members and their friends and families. Our goal was to go into the hurricane prepared, so that we could come through it positioned to support our crew and help our communities.

Three months after the storm, we asked each crew member for feedback about how we did as a company during this disaster. Overall, the results were very positive. Everyone was very grateful for our focus on their safety. Everyone also appreciated our efforts to help devastated communities, as well as our role in revitalizing the economy.

There was one piece of feedback that has stayed with me since that time. It came from a bright, young, and recently promoted district manager. It was simple, yet profound. He said, "One thing I wish we would have done differently about three weeks after the hurricane was step back and really look at everything going on. We were so focused on getting things done, I think we might have made better choices and done a few things differently if we would have stepped back and looked at the bigger picture. Had we done that, we would have had clearer heads and avoided some of the trial and error of what we were doing."

As leaders and restaurant operators, we instinctively worked day and night in the aftermath of Katrina. We operated just like you do when you are in the weeds at a restaurant. We just kept working harder and harder to dig our way out of it. With Katrina, those "weeds" were just so much bigger than all of us! We were so caught up in driving the company back to normal in this crisis that we did not think to step back to re-evaluate our entire plan, which could have been beneficial to the team. Stepping back allows you to slow down and gain a new perspective of your reality, giving you the opportunity to adjust or make new choices.

Whether it is a crisis or a shift in your life, it is important to step back in order to see all of your choices. Stepping back may give you a different perspective so you can clearly see your reality.

Making the Choice to Live Your Life with Personal Integrity

There is one very valuable gift that comes out of the *Love, Like, and Dislike Checklist*, and it relates to how you live your life. If you make this checklist a constant part of your life, you will find yourself living with a new level of integrity. The word *integrity* is derived from the Latin prefix *inter-*, meaning "one" or "whole." In applying the idea of "being whole" to your life, you should ask yourself: "Does my inside match my outside? Do my beliefs, my thoughts, and my feelings match the choices I make with respect to how I look, behave, and act?" When you are aligned, inside and out, you are living in integrity. It is a state of feeling charged up about your life, feeling great about your choices, and really loving who you are as a person. It is the essence of living a "whole" life.

Analyzing your *Love, Like, and Dislike Checklist* allows you to see where your life's aligned or misaligned. The more your life is aligned to your loves and likes, the more you are living your *whole* life with integrity. The more your life is aligned to your dislikes, the more you are living misaligned with integrity. Take another look at your *Love, Like, and Dislike Checklist*, and answer the following question: Am I living my *whole* life with integrity?

Once you see your reality and accept it, you are in the strongest position to make *the choice* to create the best shifts of your life. Choice can be powerful! Choice can empower or limit you. It is all about *choosing* to have the best shifts of your life. Sometimes, however, your beliefs may hinder your ability to make a choice. You may believe that you don't really have a choice, that it's impossible to make a choice because of certain circumstances in your life. The following stories are great examples of how beliefs can limit choices.

Limiting Beliefs: The Elephant Story

In some parts of the world, elephants in captivity learn their place in the world from a very young age; they are defined by their limitations. As babies, a heavy, metal chain is attached to one of their hind legs so they do not wander away. The chain is so heavy that if they pull too hard, they feel the pain in their leg. Not yet strong enough to break free, elephants at a very young age are taught that they can only move as far as the length of the chain. Eventually, they grow tired of pulling at the chain and stop trying altogether. They learn their limitations.

Years later, an adult elephant can be controlled by having a small, thin rope tied around its large, strong leg because the elephant no longer challenges what is holding him back. It accepts its limitations. The elephant's world is limited to the length of a chain.

Breaking Self-Limiting Barriers: The Roger Bannister Story

Before a man named Roger Bannister came along, there was a prevailing belief that no one could run a mile in under four minutes. Bannister believed differently. With great passion, purpose, and a plan, he set out to prove that a four-minute mile could be broken. On May 6, 1954, Roger Bannister ran a 3 minute and 59.4 second mile. It had never been done before. Yet, within a year of his record-breaking run, *thirty-seven* other runners had broken through the four-minute mile barrier. Just three years after Bannister accomplished what some believed to be the impossible, *three hundred* runners broke the four-minute mile.

What are the lessons of these stories? Beliefs can be very limiting. Look at your *Love, Like, and Dislike Checklist* again, and consider the chains of beliefs, feelings, or emotions that may be holding you back. Challenge them! It is your *choice* to either remain chained by your limitations or break free of your limitations—like Roger Bannister did.

Here are a few thoughts to consider about the reality of your life:

- It is your reality, and *you* have the power to make a new choice!
- You can make the choice to break your chains of limiting beliefs.
- This is just one moment in time—not your entire life. You have the power right now to make choices that will move you toward living the best shifts of your life.

To love what you do and feel that it matters—how could anything else be more fun?

—Katherine Graham

Morning Inventory:
Timeframe Inventory

o o o o o o o o o o o o o o o o o o o o o o o o o o o o o o o o o

The same thinking and behavior that got you to where you are today is not the thinking and behavior that you will need to stretch to where you want to be tomorrow!

—Famous Dave Anderson, Founder of Famous Dave's Legendary Pit Bar-B-Que Restaurants and Catering

What is the biggest secret about time management? It's that time management is *really* not about managing time; it's about managing *priorities*. Priority management is the secret weapon of successful managers. As a restaurant manager, you have priorities in every shift. Restaurant managers probably have more priorities to manage than managers in any other service business.

As a restaurant manager, you know the importance of focusing on your priorities every shift. Priorities in a shift can include making sure the prep is done before lunch, hitting service times, managing labor while delivering great service, or hitting food-cost targets while serving great food. As a leader in your restaurant, you focus your team's efforts on these priorities, too.

Those same targets or priorities for a shift are much like managing the priorities of your life. Take another look at your *Love, Like, and Dislike Checklist.* Are you managing your time or managing your priorities? If you knew where you were spending your time and compared it to what you love, like, and dislike, it would certainly provide tremendous clarity about what shifts you could make in your life. To understand how to focus on your priorities, you must understand and recognize how and where you invest your time right now.

Timeframe Inventory

Each week, you have 168 hours and can do with them what you will. Once a year, you get to cheat (if you observe daylight-savings time), and once a year, you get cheated, but other than that, you have the same timeframe to work with every week. With so much practice, you'd think you would know exactly how you spend your time—but when is that *really* the case? Well, in another 168 hours, it will be! The objective of the *Timeframe Inventory* is to track how you spend your time during an average week.

The *Timeframe Inventory* has four areas of focus for you to record your time: personal, personal connections, wealth creation, and community connections. The following definitions are provided to help you inventory your time. Consider them them as a guide to categorizing and framing your time.

In the "**personal**" timeframe, consider your habits. How many hours do you spend on activities solely for your benefit, like hobbies, relaxing, Golden Hours, exercising, sleeping, and planning your life?

In the "**personal connections**" timeframe, focus on the people in your life. How much time each week do you spend on your relationships with your significant other or spouse, your friends, or your family (for example, siblings, parents, children, and other family members)?

In the "**wealth creation**" timeframe, concentrate on your career and the ways you create financial opportunities for your life. For example, each week, how much time do you spend at your job (including commuting to work), furthering your career (networking, attending seminars and conferences, etc.), managing your budget, investing money, reducing your debt, improving your credit score, or gaining knowledge about personal finance?

In the "**community connection**" timeframe, think about the time you spend supporting and giving to others. For example, each week, how much time do you spend on community involvement, volunteering, or spiritual growth?

Each timeframe is interdependent of the others, and together they frame a whole picture of the choices that you make with your time. Try to be as accurate as possible without spending so much time that calculating time becomes a time slot! There are no right or wrong answers, so be honest with yourself. Track down those mystery hours that seem to disappear—*those* are the very ones you might soon be spending differently. Be sure that your total week adds up to 168 hours.

There are no expectations that your time will be divided equally into all four frames. Let's take sleep, for example. It falls under the personal timeframe. Unless you're a new parent, sleep alone takes roughly a third of one's day. So personal time could, for example, outweigh your community connection time. Depending on one's situation in life, personal connections might outweigh wealth creation or vice versa. Your inventory should be a reflection of where you spend your time over the course of a week.

Here are a few tips for tracking your time:

- This is not a perfect science; there is a fine balance between estimating to avoid unnecessary stress and being accurate to avoid missing things. So, for the purposes of this activity, track your time in thirty-to-sixty-minute increments (an example would be that you, on average, spend two hours a day texting).

- There are multiple ways to track your time for a week. You can:
  - use the Google Calendar application,
  - use the calendar on a PDA-type device,
  - utilize your Outlook calendar,
  - or go for the old-school method of pencil and paper.

- Here are few additional tips:
  - If you want to track your time by hours, use the daily tracker for just seven days!
  - Try to account for twenty-four hours each day.
  - Recognize that your schedule changes every week, so pick a more typical week to track. Tracking your vacation week or the week you travel for the annual conference won't be very helpful.

Thoughts for Your Timeframe Inventory

If you have never done this before, it can be overwhelming. This is a true, legitimate look at how you are doing at managing your priorities. It is intended to create awareness. Facing your reality is one of the most challenging things you will have to do in your life. *Many* people never even look at their reality. They live in denial and create habits to *keep* them in denial. However, the true power in creating the best shifts of your life is by facing your reality. In that one choice, you take control your life versus having your life control *you*!

Example of Daily Time Inventory

The following is a *Daily Time Inventory*, which is similar to your daily sales records. Your goal here is to record where you are spending your time each day. So, for example, if you sleep from midnight to six, you would write the word "sleep" under the "Personal" column.

Here is an *example* of one of my daily timeframes.

Time	Personal YOU	Personal Connections	Wealth Creation	Community Connections
Midnight	Sleep			
1:00 AM	Sleep			
2:00 AM	Sleep			
3:00 AM	Sleep			
4:00 AM	Sleep			
5:00 AM	Sleep			
6:00 AM		E-mails		
7:00 AM	Work Out			
8:00 AM	Get Ready			
9:00 AM			Client visit	
10:00 AM			Client visit	
11:00 AM			Client visit	
Noon			Client visit	
1:00 PM			Client visit	
2:00 PM			Client visit	
3:00 PM			Client visit	
4:00 PM			Client visit	
5:00 PM			Client visit	
6:00 PM			Client visit	
7:00 PM		Dinner with friends		
8:00 PM		Dinner with friends		
9:00 PM				Volunteer Emails
10:00 PM	Television			
11:00 PM	Sleep			

Your Daily Time Inventory

You can make the inventory as detailed or as simple as you'd like. The key is that it works for you!

Time	Personal YOU	Personal Connections	Wealth Creation	Community Connections
Midnight				
1:00 AM				
2:00 AM				
3:00 AM				
4:00 AM				
5:00 AM				
6:00 AM				
7:00 AM				
8:00 AM				
9:00 AM				
10:00 AM				
11:00 AM				
Noon				
1:00 PM				
2:00 PM				
3:00 PM				
4:00 PM				
5:00 PM				
6:00 PM				
7:00 PM				
8:00 PM				
9:00 PM				
10:00 PM				
11:00 PM				

Analyzing Your Weekly Timeframe Inventory Worksheet

After you have tracked your daily timeframes, transfer the information to a weekly timesheet, which is very similar to how you transfer your daily inventory reports to your weekly inventory report. Write your "collective" activities and the hours you spend on them into each one of the frames in the following worksheet.

Here is an example to help you get started.

PERSONAL		PERSONAL CONNECTIONS	
Sleep	42 hours	Visiting Friends	3 hours
Exercising	7 hours	Dinner with Family	7 hours
Reading	2 hours	Help my Cousin Move	7 hours
		Time with the Family	20 hours
		Time with my Spouse	10 hours
Total Number of Hours: 51		Total Number of Hours: 47	
WEALTH CREATION		**COMMUNITY CONNECTIONS**	
Work	40 hours	Volunteering	7 hours
Managing Finances	3 hours	Community Activity	2 hours
Travel for Work	10 hours		
Financial Management			
Seminar	8 hours		
Total Number of Hours: 61		Total Number of Hours: 9	

Analyzing Your Weekly Timeframe Inventory Worksheet

PERSONAL	PERSONAL CONNECTIONS
Total Number of Hours:	Total Number of Hours:
WEALTH CREATION	COMMUNITY CONNECTIONS
Total Number of Hours:	Total Number of Hours:

Timeframe-activity totals:
Personal   _____
Personal Connections   _____
Wealth Creation   _____
Community Connections   _____

Total Hours   168

Timeframe Inventory Evaluation

As you examine your results, here are a few questions to consider.

You can write your answer to each in the space provided.

- How many *total* hours did you spend in each timeframe?

- What were the activities or collections of activities in each timeframe that consumed large amounts of your time?

- What was your initial reaction after seeing where your hours are spent each week?

- What pleases you the most about how you are spending your time?

- What surprises you the most about how you are spending your time?

- What are your areas for the biggest opportunities and challenges?

- What choices can you make that will enable you to focus more on your priorities and reinvest your time in order to live the best shifts of your life?

Considerations for Your Timeframe Inventory

Here is the best news about your *Timeframe Inventory*: you control it! It's perfectly natural if you are pleasantly surprised by the results. Or, you may not like what you see. Either way, you are now in a position to make changes and can begin (almost) immediately!

The first time I did this, I wanted to change everything about how I was spending my time and not managing my priorities. I realized that if I started changing everything without a clear plan, without knowing where I was going, it would lead me right back to spending my time and not managing my priorities.

The key here is this: for right now, just take a breath and continue to "play through" the rest of this section; it's just like finding the kitchen in the weeds. You can clearly see everything that has to be done. Depending upon your perspective, you can panic, which only makes the situation worse; you can ignore it, which also makes the situation even worse; or you can continue to "play through to clear the board," taking it one order and one situation at a time until it is all clear.

As managers, we are trained to address and solve problems immediately. But in life, sometimes we reach our best solution by thinking it through before we make our next move. So, as you look at your timeframes, just continue to play through until everything is clear.

Align Your Weekly Timeframe Inventory with your Love, Like, and Dislike Checklist

The next move to help you gain more clarity on your reality is to invest some time exploring whether your *Timeframe Inventory* is aligned with your *Love, Like, and Dislike Checklist*. Are you making choices that focus your time on your priorities in life, or do you feel like you are just wasting your time?

Go back to the four focuses of the *Weekly Time Inventory*, and, using your *Love, Like, and Dislike Checklist*, note the amount of time that you are spending on the things you love, the things you like, and the things you dislike. Based upon your comparison, reflect on the following questions:

- Where are you spending the greatest number of hours? Are they on the things you love, the things you like, or the things you dislike?

- If you could start with a clean piece of paper, what would your ideal timeframe inventory look like?

- What shifts can you make right now to recalibrate some of your time and prioritize it on areas that you love and like?

- To prioritize more time on the areas you love, what choices are you considering making to reinvest your time?

The first time I did this comparison, I found that I was spending the least amount of my 168 hours on the things that I love. I quickly discovered most of my time was spent doing things I disliked, namely doing several aspects of my job I didn't like. I also saw that I didn't spend even one hour a week with my friends. I saw that I liked exercising, but I was spending only two hours a week doing so.

The *Timeframe Inventory* and the *Love, Like, and Dislike Checklist* gave me a great opportunity to ask myself what choices I had made to find myself in that situation. It also gave me the opportunity to ask what choices I needed to start making in order to shift my life, my time and my job to a better place. I did, after all, have choices. I could either stop sleeping completely and use those forty-two hours for a new purpose, or I could change priorities. Clearly, it was the latter. The clarity of this realization ignited my inner power to transform my life.

Changing priorities is sometimes harder than it sounds. Changing your priorities is a life-altering decision; it is not a decision that is made easily or quickly. And once you've made it, you might feel uncomfortable or uneasy for a while. Other people may not like your new priorities and may actually try to get you to hold on to the old ones. However, the key to living your best life is to align your time with your priorities and use it to reframe your life!

Reframing Your Timeframes for Your Life

This is a terrific opportunity to take a new inventory of your time. Now that you've seen what your reality looks like, take a look at what a shift in your *Timeframe Inventory* might look like. What would your life look like if you were to reframe it so that you invested more time in what you love and what you like? What would it look like if your time were aligned to the priorities of your life? In this section, have some fun; just reframe your time so that it reflects where you would invest it if you were to align it with your priorities and what you love, like, and dislike.

Reframe Your Timeframe Inventory Worksheet

PERSONAL	PERSONAL CONNECTIONS
Total Number of Hours:	Total Number of Hours:
WEALTH CREATION	**COMMUNITY CONNECTIONS**
Total Number of Hours:	Total Number of Hours:

Analyzing Your Time Utilization

What was your initial reaction when you saw where your hours are spent each week?

Timeframe Activity Totals
   1) **Personal**   _____

   2) **Personal Connections**   _____

   3) **Wealth Creation**   _____

   4) **Community Connections**   _____

   Total Hours   ___**168**___

   Throughout the course of my career, I have done this exercise many times. I have used it whenever I have made significant shifts in my life, from starting a new job to moving to a new state to balancing new responsibilities in my personal or family life.

   There is power in seeing what possibilities exist when you shift your perspective. Another way of looking at this is the same way you manage the daily inventory in your restaurant. In order to ensure that you don't run short, you regularly check the inventory. You probably don't check your inventory in a haphazard way, letting days, weeks, months go by without taking inventory. It would be constant chaos! Taking inventory is a dynamic process.

   It is no different when it comes to managing your priorities. If you never manage your priorities, your life will be in a constant state of chaos. If you make it a habit to consciously manage your priorities, just as you make it a habit to ensure that you always have the right inventory of products, you will not be limited to having to settle for just what is available or just what is in stock. You will be able to make choices based on preference rather than convenience. Imagine the menu that you could create for your life!

Your time is limited, so don't waste it living someone else's life.
Don't be trapped by dogma—which is living with the results of other people's thinking.
Don't let the noise of others' opinions drown out your own inner voice.
And most important, have the courage to follow your heart and intuition.
They somehow already know what you truly want to become.
Everything else is secondary.
—Steve Jobs

MID SHIFT

✦

MID SHIFT

Menu Development:
The Menu of Your Life

Congratulations on the completion of your opening shift! You have already made an amazing shift in gaining more clarity about your reality. Once you know where you are, it becomes very exciting to see the possibilities of where you can go.

The mid shift bridges two day parts, typically lunch and dinner. The mid shift is also the link between a successful open and a successful close. The manager lucky enough to work the mid has the pleasure of working both the lunch rush and dinner rush, and in between is usually taking on a list of projects and assignments that must get completed in the middle of the afternoon. The ability of a manager to run a "mid" can mean the success or failure of the day. The actions of the mid-shift manager impact everything and everyone for the day. Managers that work the "mid" must be clear about where they are, where they want to go, and what their plan of action is to produce results.

The mid shift is also a great representation of where you are in this book. You've looked at your reality and now it's time to focus on how to create great shifts in your life. The first step is to gain clarity on the possibilities of your life. Identifying the possibilities of your life is much like creating a menu for a restaurant. Think about managing the mid shift. You must know the menu for both lunch and dinner and be able to plan and execute them successfully. This is not unlike your menu of life; if you are clear about what you want in it, then you can similarly plan and execute a successful menu of your life too!

Take a few minutes and explore the similarities between the menu for a restaurant and a menu for your life.

Menu Development

Restaurants distinguish themselves in a variety of ways. One of the most distinctive ways is with the menu. A menu takes on a life of its own. It can represent the heart and soul of a chef/owner, a cuisine, or an entire concept. It is one of the key drivers of a successful restaurant.

At first glance, you think *how hard is it to come up with a menu?* You just put down what you enjoy cooking and what you know you're good at presenting, right? Oh—and try to avoid putting down the same things that the restaurant one block over has on its menu. In reality though, you find out that developing and executing a menu is definitely a journey and not a destination.

Think about everything that goes into menu development:
- The definition of the type of food.
- The number of items offered.
- The recipe development.
- The number of ingredients.
- The ideal food costs.
- The supply chain.
- The recipe procedures.
- The presentation standards.
- The food-safety handling.
- The customer perception of the product.
- The physical requirements for storage, preparation, and delivery.

And those steps are part of the process for just getting the food and beverage side in the development. The next part of the process is the design of the physical menu, with activities such as:
- The physical layout of the menu board or menu—how the actual menu layouts look on paper or some other type of display.
- Accentuating menu items to heighten their customer appeal.
- The visual elements of the menu to inspire purchases.
- Menu-item descriptions to create "craveable" sensations.
- Pricing to build sales and create value propositions.
- Developing limited-time offers to drive traffic.
- Implementing specials to provide diversity.
- Creating seasonal menus to promote seasonal ingredients.

- Analyzing product mixes to ensure that there is the right balance of margins and customer satisfaction.

Developing menus and menu products is a complex process; it is truly both an art and a science. It is *also* an imperfect process. Sometimes the one product that everyone loves in test is put on the menu and it bombs, while the one product that everyone questions in test is the one that takes off! Developing a menu requires doing some background research, as well as having some faith in the process. Product and consumer research processes support the decisions about menu items. Faith supports the time, effort, and investment necessary to actualize a successful product.

It can be a very daunting task to develop a menu from scratch. But menus are rarely developed overnight; they are developed over *time*. Similarly, you don't just throw your goals together; you develop them over time. And just as a restaurant menu needs continual improvement, so does your life menu. Your life menu will change over time; you will add to, subtract from, and modify it.

Creating a new menu or a new menu product is a journey that can produce amazing results. Likewise, creating and achieving life goals and dreams is a fantastic journey! What is the secret to developing a phenomenal menu? It's about starting with a vision from the beginning and driving to the ultimate outcome. The joy is when that menu hits just right—it is absolutely one of the greatest feelings in the world! Think about how that manifests itself in a restaurant chain—how amazing is it when one sandwich can be served in over twenty-six thousand restaurants in over a hundred countries. Now *that* is powerful!

Putting that into the context of your life, what does your "menu of life" look like? What is at the heart of it for you? What would you like to achieve? Where do you want to go? Essentially, your menu of life is a reflection of your goals and dreams. Sometimes, it can be very intimidating to look at your entire lifespan, so another way of looking at it can be simply to break it down by a week, a month, a year, and ultimately, a lifetime. For example, ask yourself what your goals are for this week. This month? This year? It's not easy, but this is the way to start creating your ideal life menu.

How do you know when you are ready to develop the Menu of Your Life? Take a moment to answer the following questions.

- Do you have goals in your life for the next year?
- Do you know what you want your life to become but are uncertain about how to create it?
- Are you working hard and feeling like you're going nowhere?

- Do you feel like you're under so much pressure to be successful, yet you feel stuck?
- Do you feel that if you could get a lucky break, it would change the path of your life?
- Do you feel misaligned or disconnected between what you think you should be doing and what you *are* doing?
- Do you have a constant nagging feeling that you want more out of your career?
- Would you like to shift your life to a new level?

If you answered yes to some of these questions, you are not alone. Personally, I have answered yes to every question at different times in my life. I made some shifts that propelled me forward toward my goals, and made other shifts that steered me off course. By continually developing your goals and dreams, you will become more and more aware of how to proactively create the shifts in your life.

How do you create shifts that are consistent with what you want to achieve? The easy answer is the most obvious one—you find the answer within yourself! Tapping into your personal power, your passion, and, ultimately, your personal dreams is a method to get to that place. It is the place where goals and dreams move from thoughts and ideas to actions and realities. For example, is there something that you are really passionate about? Are there goals or dreams related to this passion that you can create for yourself? Perhaps your passion is playing the drums, something you wished you did more often. Have you thought about making that happen by creating goals for yourself? Maybe your goal is to spend at least an hour on your drums every Sunday. Or perhaps it's joining a group or a local band?

For me, it's cycling; I have a passion for long-distance cycling. I decided to transform that passion into the goal of riding a "century," a hundred-mile ride in one day—the cycling equivalent to a marathon. Completing my first century was such an *amazing* experience! It was exhilarating to finish the ride; I had an overwhelming feeling of joy knowing I had achieved one of my life goals. *By translating your passion into goals and dreams, you will find that your Love, Like, and Dislike Checklists and Timeframe Inventory are more balanced, and better reflect the Menu of Your Life.*

However, it is not always easy to sit down and suddenly write down all of your goals and dreams. Often, individuals resist developing menus of their lives because of reasons ranging from "it seems too daunting" to "there isn't enough time." Or they let defeatist feelings get in the way: "Why try if I'm never going to make it happen?" Or, *"What's the point? This is my life, and I just have to accept it."*

Now, take those same obstacles and apply them to menu development in a restaurant. What if the owner or the chef said, "developing a menu seems too daunting...there isn't enough time...it's never going to happen...what's the point...let's just open the door and see how it goes." Or, "Let's just put easy, boring things on our menu—everyone loves peanut butter and jelly." How successful would that menu be?

We all get caught up in just trying to get through each day, or month, and over time, we forget about our goals and dreams. The worst dream-killer of all is: *"I don't have time for this nonsense; I have important things to do!"* Really, how much does it cost to dream? How much time does it take to invest some thought in your future? *Take the time.* It's *your* menu—it's *your* life!

Your Dream Journal

Have you given a lot of thought to your goals and dreams? Most people daydream, but not many people actually take the time to write down and develop their dreams. I didn't either until a friend suggested that I take a blank pad of paper and just start writing. I was surprised at how much I wrote—not just about work, but about other things that I wanted to accomplish in life. It was a magical feeling because, for the first time in a long time, I had expanded my vision, my goals, and my dreams. I realized that I had been so busy keeping everything going on a day-to-day basis that it had been awhile since I had invested any time in thinking about the possibilities of my dreams.

In that exercise I reconnected with the significance of dreams in my life's journey, and the importance of articulating them. It can be a creative and on-going process, not one that is overwhelming. I created what I call a *"Dream Journal,"* to capture a list of all the things I want to do in my life—big and small. There are no limits, no restrictions; it captures everything. The *Dream Journal* is like a recipe book, filled with pictures and diagrams and notes to myself. It is very powerful to be able to embrace the possibilities instead of forgetting or ignoring them.

Here are three steps to creating your own *Dream Journal*:

1. Think about everything you have always wanted to try, do, or experience.
2. Write everything down. Be as specific as possible; the more details you include, the better.
3. Review your list, and think about it throughout the course of the next several days.

Remember, your Dream Journal will always be a work in progress. Continue to add to your Dream Journal, and circle dreams and goals that become a reality. You will see recipes of your life becoming clearer and clearer.

My Dream Journal (2002)

Here is an example from my original Dream Journal:

Write a series of books on leadership, self-empowerment, and business strategy.

Create a successful international speaking platform.

Travel internationally to countries/places with my friends and family:

Hong Kong	Australia	Bahamas
Russia	Africa	Fuji
Italy	Egypt	Caribbean
Norway	Mexico	Isle of Capri

Play golf and have an average score of 85.

Play St. Andrews golf course in Scotland.

Sail on a Windjammer.

Own properties in Napa, Florida, Chicago, and internationally.

Insure my financial sustainability to support my goals and my dreams.

Support my nieces and nephews with their dreams to go to college or with their careers.

Start a scholarship at the Educational Foundation to honor my mom.

Find ways to be actively involved in my community and give back to others.

Complete a century bicycle ride.

Dream Journal

Developing the Menu of Your Life *for the Next Year*

As you are filling up your *Dream Journal* ("dream recipe book"), you are in a great place to now transfer some of your dreams and goals to create the "*Menu of Your Life*." Creating the *Menu of Your Life* is an activity that allows you to organize your dreams and goals so that you can focus on accomplishing them. It consists of two parts: first, developing your menu, and second, designing your menu.

In the first part, developing your menu, you simply want to list your goals and dreams. Some people like to write their goals and dreams for their entire life, some people for the next three years, and others select their own timeframes. I would suggest that you develop and design the *Menu of Your Life* for any period of time that best suits you! I have found that sometimes the best place to start is to develop and design your first menu for a one-year period.

Here is an effective way to organize your dreams and goals for one year. Using your *Dream Journal,* select all of the goals and dreams you would like to accomplish in the next year. To help you with the selection process, complete the following question. As you complete the sentence, start filling in the space below.

I am living the best shifts of my life when.......

Tips for Developing the Menu of Your Life

Here are my tips to support you in creating the *Menu of Your Life* for the next year:

- There are no right or wrong responses.
- Think big, dream big, and be specific about your goals and dreams.
- Realize that, sometimes, even small thoughts lead to larger dreams or goals.
- Don't worry about *how* you will achieve your dreams and goals. For the purpose of this activity, focus more on *what* your dreams *look like* versus *how* you will achieve them.
- Create timeframes for your goals and dreams. Do you want to achieve this by next week, in the next three months, or over the course of the year? Find a place and time that works best for you to give yourself the opportunity to think and be creative.
- Be open to new possibilities!

Thought Starters if you need help getting started:

Your Personal Choices

What are your dreams for your own education, hobbies, travel, or home life?

What do you want to achieve for yourself?

What are your goals for your health?

If you won the lottery and had unlimited funds, what would you do?

Your Personal Connections

What are the dreams you have related to romantic relationships? With your spouse or significant other?

What are your dreams for your family or friends?

What are your dreams for your children?

Your Wealth Creation

What do you want to achieve professionally?

What do you want to do with your career?

What do you want to achieve financially?

How much money do you want to earn annually? In ten years? Throughout your lifetime?

What do you want to do with your financial and career success?

Your Community Connections

How do you plan to give back and help others?

What type of contribution would you like to make to your community?

Designing Your Menu of Life

Once you have listed out your goals and dreams for the year, you can write them in your own *Menu of Life*. Simply transfer your goals and dreams to the following worksheet, so that you have an everyday visual of what you want for your life. Carry it with you—keep it on your laptop or PDA or any other place that would allow you to read it every day.

Personal	Personal Connections
Wealth Creation	Community Connections

The Menu of My Life

Here is a partial overview of my menu from 2002. (Please note this was for more than one year!)

Personal

I am healthy, active, and fit.

I have an abundance of energy, and I love biking and walking.

I am content, I am at peace, and I am spiritually fulfilled.

I am fulfilling my purpose—to positively impact others to ignite the power within in order to live the best shifts of their lives!

I am actively managing my professional goals with my personal goals.

Personal Connections

I am in a personal relationship that is loving, supportive, and filled with joy.

I am at peace with all of my relationships. In fact, they have never been better.

I am surrounded by friends and colleagues who support and believe in my vision.

I am visiting my family back home a minimum of every six weeks.

I am staying connected with friends on a more consistent basis.

Wealth Creation

I build a business to support individuals and organizations to get to the next level of success.

I travel internationally, speaking for business and philanthropic initiatives.

I am an international authority on leadership, self-fulfillment, and building great organizations.

I am the author of a series of books on leadership, self-fulfillment, and building great organizations.

I have financial freedom for the rest of my life so I can continue to create and give back to others.

Community Connections

I am giving back purposefully to our society through volunteer work.

I have developed my own foundation to find cures and help people with cancer.

I am giving away a percentage of my annual income to charitable organizations.

I am supporting my local community by being involved in organizations that I am passionate about and that are making a difference.

Vision Board

A vision board is another way to design a *Menu of Your Life*. You know all about the importance of writing down your goals, and you've probably heard of the power of visualizing your success. Many elite athletes find that visualization helps; they imagine their success before it happens. Visualization creates strong images in your mind that can support your focus in life.

Vision boards are created through the use of items you probably already have in your home. These include magazines, articles, catalogs, newspapers, pictures, or other materials that represent something to you. The objective of the vision board is to create your own collage that reflects all of your goals and dreams by utilizing pictures, words, textures, colors, and your imagination.

Creating a vision board is a way to express the *Menu of Your Life* with the full flare of your creativity. It is an excellent way to combine your goals with the techniques of visualization. Vision boards also allow you to bring clarity to your goals and serve as a powerful illustration of the possibilities of your life!

Here's how to get started:
1. Pull together all of your supplies. This can include tape, glue, glitter, ribbon, string, fabric, markers, photos, magazines, and anything else that you would like to add to your board.
2. Identify your board. This can be cardboard, plasterboard, plywood, or something as simple as poster board. Select the size of board that bests suits your dreams and goals.
3. Lay out your vision board. Start cutting and positioning visual illustrations of your goals and dreams. You can organize by theme—personal, personal connections, wealth creation, and community connections.
4. Think of how you would like your life to look in the next year. Start making it a reality by gluing, pasting, and taping your vision together in a way that speaks to you!
5. After you have it constructed, highlight your most important image, then paint, draw, or include inspiring words that describe who you are and who you are striving to become in your life. Find a happy photo of yourself, and add it to the board.
6. Keep your board where it can serve as a daily visual reminder of the Menu of Your Life.

Cultivating and Nurturing Your Dreams

Mark Twain once said, *"Keep away from people who try to belittle your ambitions. Small people always do that, but the really great make you feel that you, too, can become great."*

It is important to realize that at first your goals and dreams are vulnerable pieces of who you are, so you need to protect them. It is important that you give them an opportunity to become stronger and clearer to increase the probability of them becoming a reality. Imagine that your dreams are like a balloon, floating high and lifting you up higher and higher. You must protect them because in a moment, your balloon can be popped, and you can fall right back to earth. Dreams and goals, if not protected, can be shattered with one fear or one sharp criticism taken deeply to the heart.

Always nurture your dreams. Sometimes, after creating the *Menu of Your Life*, you may be lifted up, as if by a balloon, and want to rush out and share your new clarity with friends and family. They might say, "This is fantastic! Go for it! I know that you can do it," "I love you so much, and I believe in you so much," or "If anyone can live the best shift of their life, it is you."

Or, instead of enthusiastic encouragement, you might hear, "Well, *that* sounds interesting, but why don't you wait until you've finished what you are doing right now?" Or you might hear, "That's one of those things that sounds great—until you do it." Or you might hear the ultimate one: "Why did you bother going to school if *that's* all you really want to do?"

Your friends and family love you, want to protect you, and do not want to see your balloon popped. They are afraid you will get hurt or disappointed, so they burst your dream before it can happen on its own. It is an ironic twist that in trying to protect you, they may leap in to cause the disappointment they fear.

Some friends and family members may also have a deep-rooted fear that if you change, you will leave them and the comfort zone within your relationship. They may be afraid of changing and pursuing their dreams, so your shift can actually make them realize their own fears and inadequacies.

If you sense that their fear is going to bring you down rather than challenge you in a helpful way, don't get bogged down in defending your dream to them; this isn't a constructive discussion. Thank them for their concerns, and move forward. Have some handy phrases ready, such as "I see what you're saying, and I'll keep that in mind," or "I'll have to look into that," then make a note not to share these ideas with them again until your balloon is already soaring.

Early on, the first time I completed my *Dream Journal* and the *Menu of My Life*, I shared my *Dream Journal* with someone I trusted who was very close to me. My intent in sharing this was to help him gain clarity about his own *Menu of Life*. I was so excited to share my goals, dreams, and newfound sense of clarity. I was convinced that sharing it would be so great for him too.

However, instead of getting encouragement and affirmation, he infused my dreams with doubt and criticism; he made fun of what I had written down. I could have kicked myself for sharing before I was ready. In one sharp comment, he made me feel as though my dreams had been popped.

I learned quickly that in order for my dreams to really soar, I needed to nurture and cultivate them first and allow them to grow firmly into a reality. I also needed to share my dreams with people who would not only support me, but who would also keep me focused on my realities. I didn't let this experience dissuade me from sharing my dreams and goals with people. I did realize I needed to be mindful about who I shared my dreams and goals with as I was nurturing them to reality.

Your Personal Board of Directors

One very effective way to nurture and grow your dreams and goals is to assemble a personal board of directors. Your personal board of directors is your "Life Board." Your Life Board should support you in good times and bad. They love and care about you, and they *support* your dreams and goals instead of *fear* them. The benefit of your personal board of directors is that they come from a position of wanting the best for you. Their role is to provide honest and direct feedback and not judge you. They know you well as a person, and they hold you accountable for your strengths, your weaknesses, and everything in between.

I began sharing my dreams and goals with a small group of people as my dreams and goals became clearer and more solidified. Today, my board consists of my sisters, trusted friends, and several close business associates. The group is incredibly diverse in age, gender, background, and geography. The one commonality is that I trust them implicitly. I have shared the life of my dreams with them during every step of the way. They hold me accountable and support me in my choices.

Think about it from a restaurant perspective: most great companies have strong, diverse boards. Companies look for outside opinions and insights, too! In fact, there are often very rigorous procedures for *qualifying* to be a board member. When you think about your personal board of directors, what types of qualifications are you looking for in your board? This has to be a group of people that have the self-confidence and courage to provide you objective and positive feedback, even when it is not what you may want to hear.

Creating your personal board of directors is an amazing tool that can help you focus on making your dreams and goals become your reality. Here are a few steps towards creating your own personal board of directors.

- Select individuals that you respect and admire. These might be friends, family members, mentors, or individuals in business or your community. The key is having people you trust and respect on your board.

- Try over time to develop a diverse board of directors, because it provides diverse perspectives in supporting your choices and the shifts of your life. A personal board of directors is your "inner circle." They are connected to you, informally and formally, as you move forward in your life's journey. You can connect with them individually, in small groups, or, if you feel the need, all together.

- Your personal board of directors does not need to be large. My first board only had three people on it. The key is quality over quantity. Your objective for having them on your board is to provide support, insight, and wisdom for you as you pursue your dreams and goals.

- Be clear in your expectations for your board of directors, and make sure *they* are clear about your expectations. I expect my personal board of directors to:
  - support me in living the best shifts of my life;
  - ask me tough and thought-provoking questions;
  - challenge my process to ensure that I've really thought through my plans;
  - celebrate my successes; and
  - serve as a sounding board for my life.

- Realize that board members come and go as you journey through the shifts of your life. As you build your board, some members will stay with you for your lifetime, others will be a part of it for a specific purpose or period of time, and some members may not meet your expectations at all. I have had several board members with me from the beginning. Several of my personal board members have never even met each other. Some were only a part for a short time. No matter the length of the time or reason for the departure, I valued all of the support that they provided me.

- I have never had an official meeting of my board of directors. They are individuals I call, email, or connect with one-on-one at different stages of my life to support me in achieving my goals and dreams.

- Be reciprocal with board members (and others). If you ask someone to be on your personal board of directors, then be willing to participate on another's board. I am very fortunate that I have been asked to sit on many personal boards as a mentor, as a coach, and as a friend.

- Build your board of directors now! List two people you are certain will be supportive of you with no judgment. These are the first candidates for your personal board of directors. Add to your board over time as your journey becomes clearer.

Champions aren't made in the gym. Champions are made from something they have deep inside them—a desire, a dream, a vision. They have to have last-minute stamina; they have to have the skill and the will. But the will must be stronger than the skill.

—Muhammed Ali

Working Lunch:
Clarifying Your Life's Purpose

○ ○

Believe in your dream. People may tell you that you won't make it, that you're wasting your time. If you keep your dream in mind, have done your research and are willing to work hard, you can make it come true.

—Dave Thomas, Founder of Wendy's International

I always loved working the lunch rush all the way back in my days as a cashier at McDonald's. Talk about the ultimate adrenaline rush. A great lunch rush brings out such an amazing sense of accomplishment, teamwork, and success for everyone on the shift. I think the lunch rush is an excellent example of where passion and purpose converge to deliver an incredible result. A successful mid-shift manager focuses the passion and purpose of the team to deliver great lunch and dinner rush results. This may be similar to where you are right now in your journey through this book. You know your goals and dreams from the *Menu of Your Life* and now it is a question of harnessing your passion and purpose to achieve it!

What is Passion?

Passion is your unconditional love for something—something that you would do for free because you love it so much. Passion is this incredible energy that you have about something that is very important in your life. Or said differently, passion is like fuel for your car. You can have the fastest car in the world; however, without fuel, it is going nowhere.

Through the years, people have shared with me what they are most passionate about, like spending time with their family, improving their golf game, learning how to speak a new language, their career, being a cake decorator, specialty gardener, skateboarding champion, gourmet food expert, etc. In fact some people have multiple passions. Your passion is a very personal choice.

Having clarity about your passion will serve as a building block for having clarity about your purpose. Going back to the fuel and car example: passion is the fuel for your car and purpose is your car. The combination of the two can take you anywhere. The key is to have clarity about both and understand the significance of the combination to make you unstoppable!

Here are a few thought starters around passion to support you in identifying your passion or clarifying your passion.

- If you won the lottery tomorrow, what would you immediately do differently in your life?

- What would you do full-time for free if you knew all of your bills and living expenses were taken care of?

- Does your passion fit into your life today? If so, how?

- How do you share your passion with others?

- Does your passion benefit the greater good?

Why is Purpose Important?

Purpose, like passion, is very personal and unique to you. Think about it this way: passion is your love and enthusiasm for something. But passion with no purpose is a lot of excitement and energy without any real direction. Understanding your own unique purpose is a true gift of life.

There are three fundamental elements for understanding purpose:

1. The greatest opportunity in life is finding your purpose and living with purpose.
2. Many believe our purpose is to serve a higher power, the universe, and/or the greater good of humanity. Another way of looking at this is to think of purpose as providing the "whys" in your life. Creating the best shifts of your life becomes more relevant when you understand *why* you are driven in your life and how that translates to the shifts of your life. Living the best shifts of your life becomes more relevant when you understand what your purpose is and how it contributes to the greater whole.
3. Identifying your purpose takes time and attention. It requires choice, commitment, and effort. The key is to understand that your purpose will evolve over time and that it is definitely not a project; it is a life process.

Cornerstone of Your Purpose: Your Values and Beliefs

Identifying Your Values and Your Beliefs

Values are ideals that are important to you. I value personal integrity, freedom of speech, honesty, directness, and hard work. Your values reflect who you are inside. Values serve as an important part of the foundation of your purpose.

Beliefs are things you accept to be true. I believe that every person has the potential to contribute to the greater good, regardless of his or her circumstances. Beliefs are based upon the ability to trust the existence of something without proof; they evolve with experience and knowledge.

Values and beliefs serve as the cornerstone for your purpose. Your values and beliefs shape the way you see yourself, your world, and your goals and dreams. The more positive you are about your values and beliefs, the more positive outcomes you will achieve. The more limiting you are about your values and beliefs, the more limited your outcomes will be. Values and beliefs are very powerful in shaping and directing your purpose.

Think about the power of beliefs in your restaurant: Say you hire a new server and his or her first few days do not go very well. Soon, other servers who work with the new server believe you made a bad hire. That belief gets picked up by the rest of the team. Suddenly, every time the new server has a misstep, it only continues to reinforce that the new server was a bad hire. Over time, even if the new server improves dramatically, there is still a prevailing belief that she or he was a bad hire. The new server's ultimate success is limited by the beliefs of the team until the team reevaluates its beliefs or the server quits.

Ask yourself the following questions as you think about your values and beliefs:

- What are your values? Why are these values so important to you?
- Do you speak, live, and work by your values?
- What are your beliefs? Your beliefs can be about life, things you think about the world, business, or things that are just important to you for a happy life.
- What is your perspective as you view your values and beliefs? What is influencing your view? Do you see things positively, negatively, or indifferently? There is a great saying "Your attitude determines your altitude." What is your altitude?

Values and Beliefs Activity

Completing the following activity will give you more clarity on your current values and beliefs.

Write down the values and beliefs supporting you in your life. Feel free to simply make a list or to write statements. You will find examples of values and beliefs below.

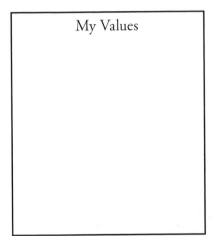

My Values	My Beliefs

Here are some examples of **VALUES:** (use this list and select which values you can relate to, or add to this list)

_____ Accountability	_____ Caring	_____ Contribution
_____ Courage	_____ Education	_____ Excellence
_____ Fairness	_____ Fun	_____ Happiness
_____ Health	_____ Honesty	_____ Individuality
_____ Integrity	_____ Passion	_____ Power
_____ Quality	_____ Service	_____ Uncompromising
_____ Trust	_____ Wealth	_____ Work Ethic

Here are some examples of my **BELIEFS:**

- I believe that every man, woman, and child has the right to be free.
- I believe that we all have the power to change our lives for the better.
- I believe that everyone has the potential for unlimited success.
- I believe that the restaurant industry is one of the greatest industries in the world.
- I believe that your network is equal to your net worth.
- I believe that life is short and you should live your life to the fullest.
- I believe that if you plan your work and work your plan, great things will happen.
- I believe that at any time in a person's life, he or she can create great shifts!

Defining Your Purpose

Defining your purpose can seem like a huge task because of the significance it plays in your life. There are many ways to define your purpose. One way I've found helpful when coaching managers to define their purpose is to begin by breaking it down into more digestible pieces. The following is a process I have used through my career, as well as with executives and managers, to create a path to identifying their purpose.

Take some time to answer the questions below:

A) **Your Passion (using your responses from earlier in this section might be helpful)**
- What are you most passionate about in the whole world?

- What would you do full-time for free if you knew all of your bills and living expenses were taken care of?

- Does your passion fit into your life today? If so, how?

- How do you share your passion with others?

- Does your passion benefit the greater good?

Sometimes in writing responses, themes or common thoughts will appear. Recurring comments, words, or thoughts could point to a central message. Do you see a common theme under Passion? If so, write it down in the space below.

B) Explore Your Successes
1. What do you believe you have been the most successful at in your life?

2. What successes are you most proud of in your life?

3. What successes would you still like to achieve?

Do you see a common theme under Success? If so, write it down in the space below.

C) Focus on Your Core Values
Refer back to the *values* and *beliefs* you have identified and please select the top three values that best capture your "core" values.

1) ————————————————

2) ————————————————

3) ————————————————

D) Identify Your Core Beliefs
Refer back to the values and beliefs you have identified, and please select your two or three "core" beliefs that really capture the essence of your beliefs.

E) Contributions
1. What contributions to people, society, or our planet will occur because you are living your life true to your passions?
2. How will people's lives improve if you make your contribution?
3. Do you see a common theme under Contributions? If so, write it down in the space below.

Your Life's Purpose Statement

1. What is the theme of your **passion**?

2. What is the theme of your **success**?

3. What are your three **core values**?

4. What are your two or three **core beliefs**?

5. What is the theme of your **contribution**?

Now, taking the combination of all of your responses and all the exercises in this book into account, try to draft one statement that would capture the essence of all your responses. The first time I did this, I wrote and rewrote my statement several times. The objective is to pull out ideas or thoughts from all your responses and develop a statement that can serve as your "purpose statement." Your purpose statement answers "why" you are driven each day when you wake up to make a shift in your life.

Go back to being the mid-shift manager at lunch: your purpose as the mid-shift manager is to support and lead the team through a successful lunch. In that process, you create a better workplace for your team and deliver a great dining experience for your customers. Identifying your purpose statement is a lot like learning to run a great lunch rush; it takes time and attention. The good news is you will make it through!

Please write your purpose statement in the space below:

Having clarity about your life's purpose is so energizing! It can serve as your compass when it becomes the centerpiece of your life. What used to be the barely acknowledged driving force in your life is now a clear guide, available at all times to help you make decisions, stay true to yourself and support the best shifts of your life.

Here is the important key: your life's purpose represents where you are *today*. As you continue to experience and journey through life, your purpose will continue to evolve. It is a good practice to check your purpose every year.

Moving Forward and Identifying Your Purpose

Finding and living your purpose is a process, not a project; everyone's purpose is unique. Defining your purpose means taking the time to find the right thoughts to crystallize it. Does that mean that you cannot move forward with your life if you do not have clarity about your purpose? Absolutely not! Of course you can move forward; just incorporate defining your purpose into the journey of your life. Have fun exploring the possibilities of your purpose.

If you get stuck right now defining your purpose exercises, take a break and try different approaches to identifying your purpose. For example, begin with the end in mind. Where do you see yourself? In his bestselling book, *Seven Habits of Highly Effective People*, Steven Covey asserts that "effective people begin with the end in mind" (Covey, 2004). As you ponder your purpose, think about your ultimate end result or dream and then work backwards to your beginning today.

Here are a few tips:
- Stay open, and invest time in answering the questions in the activity.
- Read books about purpose to expand your self-awareness.
- Ask your personal board of directors to provide insight.
- Use your Golden Hour to think about your purpose.
- Step away from the process and give yourself space and time to uncover the direction of your purpose.

- Lastly, don't get discouraged while you are clarifying your own purpose if you don't readily see it. Here is a purpose you can use that benefits everyone—the Golden Rule: "Treat others as they would like to be treated."

My friend Richard Damien gave me words of wisdom one time when I was at a stage of evolving my purpose: "Out of nothing, you will create your truth." Remain open to the possibilities of your purpose!

Most people are searching for happiness. They're looking for it. They're trying to find it in someone or something outside themselves. That's a fundamental mistake. Happiness is something that you are, and it comes from the way you think.

—Wayne Dyer

Prepping for Dinner:
Creating a Life-Shift Plan

Go for it! It is an incredible industry, filled with the most hospitable and gracious people and abundant opportunity.

—Julia Stewart, Chairman and CEO of DineEquity, Inc. and Founder of Women's Foodservice Forum

After the lunch rush, the mid-shift manager is typically charged with a list of activities between the hours of 2:00 pm and 4:30 pm. The mid-shift manager must prioritize everything that needs to be accomplished, while also ensuring that the restaurant is set up for a successful dinner. Successful mid-shift managers plan their work and work their plan.

The success of the mid shift depends upon the manager's ability to identify priorities and then develop and implement a plan for success. The mid-shift manager's strategy for success can also be utilized to achieve success in life—plan your success, and work your plan for success!

Several things happened to me after I developed my *Menu of Life* and gained even greater clarity about my purpose. I experienced a greater sense of calmness about what I wanted in my life, an excitement about the choices that I wanted to make in my life immediately, and an anticipation of what the next step would be. I wanted to understand how to move from where I was to where I wanted to be. Again, it was time for more shifts.

Tom Peters once said, "In the greatest amount of chaos is the greatest amount of change." This quote captures the truest moment in the middle of change: chaos is everywhere, and you might start to question if what you are doing is the right thing. Turning back and staying with the status quo might seem like the best idea; however, if you are really going to shift your life and see it in a new place, it is at this very moment of truth that you have to make the choice to move forward. The only option to take is to keep moving forward.

When you are making shifts in your life, just like in a restaurant, there is always an open, a middle, and a close. At this point, you are definitely in the middle of a transformational change, and you have three choices: go back, stand still, or move forward. If you choose to go back, what would the advantage be? You already know you did not want to be there, which is why you are making the choice to create shifts in your life.

The challenge of standing still is like the challenge of standing on double yellow lines on a busy street: it is only a matter of time before you will get hit. When you do get hit, you lose control and have no idea of the direction in which you are going. One of my favorite sayings is: "It's about progress, not perfection." It's better to fail moving forward than to stand still and get hit. Believe in yourself, believe in the *Menu of Your Life*, and believe in your passion and purpose. By moving forward, you can make tremendous shifts in your life. Make it an exciting and exhilarating shift forward!

This is your opportunity to move forward! Develop and implement your own *Life-Shift Plan*!

Please use the *Life-Shift Plan* template to complete the following activity.

1. Choose a dream or goal from the *Menu of Your Life* or use the dream or goal from your One Dream Activity. Select one that you feel passionate about and that is easily attainable. Be as specific and as detailed as possible in writing down your dream and goal. Try to select something that you would like to accomplish in the next thirty days.

2. Using your *Love, Like, and Dislike Checklist*, select everything that you love about your life that supports this dream and goal. What adjustments do you need to make to your *Love, Like, and Dislike Checklist* to make this dream and goal a reality?

3. Review your *Timeframe Inventory*. How will you manage your priorities to make your dream and goal a reality? Identify and adjust your timeframe to support and reinforce your dream and goal.

4. How does your life's purpose support your dream/goal?
    Answer the following questions: How do you intend to realize your dream? What positive thoughts will you focus on to support you? How will your values and beliefs inspire and motivate you to succeed? How will your passion fuel it?

5. Complete the action timeline section of the *Life-Shift Plan* to see how you will achieve your dream/goal. Include the following in your action timeline:
    What specific action steps do you need to complete to achieve your dream/goal? Assign due dates so you hold yourself accountable for accomplishing each step toward your dream/goal.

6. Identify the resources you will need to achieve your dream/goal.

7. Keep notes of each step, and record what works, so you can apply it to your next action step or *Life-Shift Plan*.

8. Have fun creating your *Life-Shift Plan* to achieve your dream/goal!

Creating a Life-Shift Plan

My Dream/ Goal Please write your dream in the space provided here.	Immediate Actions What do I want to accomplish right now?	One Week What do I want to ccomplish in the next 7 days?	One Month What do I want to accomplish in the next 30 days?
My Objectives What are the objectives I want to accomplish in this time period to achieve my dream/goal?			
Skills and Knowledge to Be Learned What, specifically, do I need to learn? What skills do I need to work on?			
Resources What resources do I need?			
Support What support do I need?			
Outcomes What outcomes do I want to achieve?			

Celebrate Your Success. Realize Your Dream/Goal.

Once you have achieved your first dream or goal, choose another one and keeping creating great shifts. Continue to utilize everything you have done and apply it to another dream and goal. If you choose to continue, realizing your dreams will become one of your greatest habits. Enjoy your dream and goal, and look forward to achieving your next one.

Fear Factor

Creating shifts in your life is an exhilarating process; however, there are times when it can also bring up other emotions, like anxiety, anxiousness, fear of the unknown, and uncertainty. As much as you want each shift to be perfect, you know that, just like in your restaurant, it doesn't always work that way. The beauty of shifts in life is that they are dynamic, constantly moving and always evolving.

In my work, I have seen many great people write a solid *Life-Shift Plan*, but they can't make it happen. The number-one reason: fear! The fear of the unknown paralyzes them. They start having thoughts like, *What happens if I start focusing on priorities and having shifts in my life? What will happen to me? What if I start to achieve my goals—then what? What if through this process, I become someone else, and I lose what I am most comfortable with in my current life?* All these are great questions—but these are all questions that come from fear!

Fear has fewer opportunities to manifest itself in you when your path is clear. Fear clouds your ability to see the shifts of your life. Fear creates doubt in your beliefs that you can achieve new shifts. Fear manifests itself in questions like "What if I can't do it?" "What if my friends and family leave me if I become a different person?" "What if I try and then fail?" and "What if I succeed and then discover I didn't want it?"

New life shifts, just like new restaurant shifts, can invite very legitimate fear. The larger your shifts, the more potential for fear to enter, creating doubt and even paralyzing you!

What fears do you have about living the best shift of your life? Write down your fears below by finishing the following question.

My fear is that if I choose to live the best shift of my life, then …

The more you confront your fear, the less control it has over you. Fear is only as great as the power you give it. As you journey through this book, leave your fears behind using the *FEAR Extinguisher*.

The FEAR Extinguisher

The best way to deal with fear is to stop it before it stops you! The *FEAR Extinguisher* is another quick tool to support you on your journey toward the best shifts of your life. Understanding the fear that holds you back is as important to the process as gaining clarity about what you want. In order to extinguish your fear, you need to recognize your fear, redirect your energy and emotion around it, take action to move away from it, and leverage the power within you to make the shifts of your life.

The most powerful way to extinguish fear is to break it down into its pieces.

F represents the **facts**. What is really the truth? Another way of looking at it is, what is the most objective perspective you have in this situation?

E represents "**e-motion**"—energy in motion. Think of the positive outcome you want, and put your nervous energy into motion to attain it.

A represents **action**. Make a definitive and committed plan to move away from your fear.

R represents **results**. What is the specific habit you will create, and how will you measure your success?

Combining the Facts, the E-motion, the Action, and the Results creates your FEAR Extinguisher. Once you break fear into its pieces, you are now ready to extinguish it!

Your FEAR Extinguisher in Action
Using the steps within the FEAR Extinguisher helped me clarify my steps to positively leave one of my jobs after evaluating the results of my *Love, Like and Dislike Checklist*. I realized that I was so grateful for my opportunities at the company; however, there was more I wanted to achieve in my career. Here is how I extinguished my fear so I could make an amazing shift in my life.

*F represents the **facts**.*
Facts, in this sense, are about your perception of yourself or your world.

What is really the truth about my FEAR (both rational and irrational)?
My fear was about being a quitter. I equated leaving my job with not completing the goals I had set forth for myself when I had originally taken the position. Would the team perceive me as a quitter, a failure, or a person who did not have the skill set to be successful in my position?

Here are some of the facts about my situation.

1. People leave jobs all the time to pursue new opportunities.
2. I had made significant contributions to the organization during my tenure.
3. I was leaving the organization in a much better place for its ongoing growth, because of the leadership I had provided while I was there. Everyone is replaceable in an organization, even when the individual does not believe that to be true.

*E represents **e-motion**—short for "energy in motion." Put your energy in motion to receive a positive outcome. Here is how I put e-motion into my decision:*

1. I wanted to inspire confidence, and I became clear about how to do this by asking questions, and having discussions with my personal board of directors, and being introspective about the benefits to both the organization and myself if I left. I also wanted to be calm and confident in my departure. I shared my plan with my family to discuss any expected and unexpected responses to my decision to leave.
2. I wanted to minimize doubts and concerns of others. I thought of how my departure would impact all of the people I interacted with, and I wanted to make sure I had taken all of their needs into consideration.
3. I prepared my plan of action to create momentum as I moved forward and through the transition.

*A represents **action**. Make a definitive and committed choice to move away from your fear. I did a number of things to accomplish this.*

1. I strategically prepared my exit plan to be as minimally disruptive to the organization as possible.

2. I wrote my own personal development plan and clearly knew what my next steps would be after I left the organization. The *Life-Shift Plan* is an excellent tool for this too.
3. I planned my resignation conversation and developed supporting messages, so I was confident and considerate of other people's doubts and concerns.
4. I scheduled several meetings with my new company thirty days after my resignation, so I had something concrete to transition to after I took some time off to re-charge.

*R represents **results**. What are the specific changes you will create, and how will you measure your success?*

1. I wanted a seamless and successful transition plan from my position to my new opportunity.
2. I wanted the organization to be set up for continued success prior to, and after, my departure.
3. I wanted to be taking on projects with my new company within six months of my departure.

Did I extinguish my fears and concerns and achieve my goal of successfully leaving my position? Yes! It was attainable, because my fear was broken into fundamental pieces and redirected into positive actions with measurable results. Were there still moments of fear that crept in again? Yes, because I am human; however, they were always quickly extinguished.

Fear often seems insurmountable; however, through the process of breaking it into manageable and measurable steps and examining what fuels your fear, you can extinguish the fear preventing you from shifting your life. Utilizing the *FEAR Extinguisher*, you can make changes to live the best shifts of your life.

Use the *FEAR Extinguisher* model to extinguish the fear you wrote in the space above.

Step 1: Face Your Fear
What is the worst thing that could happen if you made new choices to focus on your priorities today?

What benefits would you realize if you made the choice to focus on your priorities?

Step 2: E-Motion—Energy in Motion

How would you change the way you manage your priorities in order to accomplish your shift?

What would positively reinforce this shift change?

Step 3: Action with Commitment

What choices must you make or things must you do differently right now?

Utilize the *Life-Shift Plan* to lay out your course of action to extinguish your fears.

Step 4: Results—Specific and Measurable

Here is a framework for writing something specific and measurable.

I want to spend _____ hours doing the following actions:
a.
b.
c.
to accomplish the following shift in my life_____.

Take the steps you detailed on the *FEAR Extinguisher* worksheet, and apply them immediately in your *Life-Shift Plan* in the next seven days. At the end of the seven-day period, see what has changed in your life. Extend it to thirty days, and challenge yourself to transform your choice to a lifelong habit. How much better your life would be if fear were not a part of it. Fear does not have to control the best shifts of your life!

Achievement seems connected with action. Successful men and women keep moving. They make mistakes, but they don't quit.

—Conrad Hilton

CLOSING SHIFT

✦

CLOSING SHIFT

7) Closing Checklist   ROOTines for Success
8) Closing Paperwork   Giving Back Action Plan

Closing Checklist: ROOTines for Success

When you're green, you're growing. When you're ripe, you rot.

—Ray Kroc, Founder of McDonald's Corporation

The Significance of Routines

Delivering consistent results is a reflection of consistently using routines. Think about one of your best shifts. What made it so powerful? Think about athletes winning gold medals at the Olympics: are those just chance experiences, or are they the result of practicing routines over and over? You use checklists in your restaurants as a way to establish routines. You can also create powerful shifts in your life by utilizing new routines!

What is the difference between a manager who occasionally has a great shift and a manager who has great shifts the majority of the time? The great managers have routines, and then, depending on what happens, they adjust accordingly. They manage *to* the exception versus managing *by* exception. Think about when you are managing the closing shift—there are typically two major routines. One routine is to physically shut down the restaurant, and the other routine is to complete all of the closing paperwork. What routines do you have in your life? Do you have a daily routine, an exercise routine, or a routine to get the kids to and from school and their activities?

Routines in both your restaurant and your life are excellent systems to support your success in both areas. Some managers might think that routines are boring. Successful people have routines because they support the desire to deliver consistent and successful results. Having a system to support your growth is a powerful tool for achieving success with the shifts of your life.

From ROOTs to Fruits

How does a seed grow into a fruit-producing tree? The seed sprouts and slowly develops roots. These roots take hold, and the tree begins to develop from the inside out. The roots must be deep, healthy, strong, and they must grow in fertile soil. They must also have water and sun to allow the seed to reach its ultimate purpose: growing into an abundant fruit tree.

How does the growth cycle of a fruit tree apply to your life goals and dreams? Your dreams and goals are the "seeds" you have planted for what you would like to achieve in your life. In order for your dreams and goals to become a reality, they must have a strong system for support. That system is the creation of your *ROOTines*.

A strong *ROOTine* creates the ideal environment for your fruit—your life's dreams—to flourish. It supports you in becoming the strongest tree possible, so that you may deliver an abundance of fruit. Look at it this way: choosing great soil allows your roots to really take hold and is similar to selecting a terrific personal board of directors who will ground you too. Encouraging the roots to really grow deep is like nourishing and cultivating your dreams and goals. The stronger your roots, the greater your ultimate fruits will become as you grow.

As a tree grows, it reaches toward the sun, and the sun, in turn, helps the tree grow. The sun that your tree reaches for is the clarity of your reality. The more clarity you have, the more light there is for you to make choices that will grow strongly in your life.

Even the strongest trees face challenges and obstacles. Lightning can strike a tree at any time. What will your response be when you are jolted by lightning? Remember, you now have your *FEAR Extinguisher* to help you put out any potential fires!

Growing and Maintaining a Healthy Tree!

Perseverance is a key ingredient for growing and maintaining a healthy "tree." Think about when you were first learning how to run a shift in your restaurant; those first several solo shifts just flew by, and so much seemed to happen on every shift. If you were like me, there were days when you were ready to go back at it again, and other days when you didn't know if you would ever have a smooth shift. How did you and I ultimately learn how to run smooth shifts? It's simple: we learned the *routines* of shift management.

You learn routines so that you can focus on producing results, improving your effectiveness, and running more efficient shifts. It is in those times when everything is firing on all cylinders that you run your best shifts. Over time, you actually start to improve your ability to replicate great shifts. You learn more about the details, you pick up little tips, or you elevate your game to a whole new level. Then, one day, that shift happens inside you, and you are now running effective and successful shifts over and over. It is at this point that you have truly mastered your *ROOTine!*

Those same moments of learning how to master shift routines are very similar to mastering life-shift routines. They require focus, practice, and experience. They require the pursuit of life shifts that elevate your life to a new level or a new place of accomplishing a dream or goal. Two key elements in growing and maintaining healthy *ROOTines* are *sustaining your commitment* and *understanding the significance of the urgent and important.*

Sustaining Your Commitment

Life *does* happen and sometimes even your best *Life-Shift Plans*, your best habits, and your best *ROOTines* can fall to the wayside. This is not the end of the world; this is life. The question is, what is your response when your life shift does not go as planned? What is your response when you don't quite get the life shift you are looking for, even though you've told everyone what you are going to do? These can clearly be challenging moments, and there is power in how you respond to them.

Think about this example: have you ever made the decision to go on a diet? If you are like me, you have probably made this commitment more times than you care to think about. If you're fortunate enough to have never had to diet, perhaps you have tried to change some other habit to improve your health.

Once you have made the decision to diet, you begin to tell your friends and family the details. You reinforce your commitment at every meal. You are clear about what you are going to do and how it will happen. You stay steadfast in your decision. Then you go to a party and you make a decision to "cheat" on your diet. The next day, everyone is going out to brunch, and so you "cheat" just a little more. After a period of time, you begin rationalizing your cheating. You started out trying to lose fifteen pounds; after the party, you decided twelve would be good; after brunch, you think ten is not so bad. Then, after another week of cheating on your diet, you decide that five pounds is still very admirable. Then, after two weeks of cheating on your diet, you make the decision that you look great just as you are, and all of this dieting really has been a waste of time.

I know it; I have been there and done that over hundreds of pounds throughout the years. What is the missing link between achieving my goal and rationalizing it to nothing? Yes—commitment!

Commitment to your *ROOTine*—to *any ROOTine*—is a critical factor in achieving goals and dreams. Everyone can say that they are going to accomplish X; however, only a few will ever actually achieve it. The difference between the talkers and the achievers is commitment to their *ROOTine*.

Creating the best shifts of your life requires your commitment to truly making the shift. I am often asked why people give up on *ROOTines*.

Here are a few answers:
- Lack of clarity
- Lack of a plan
- Lack of support
- Lack of patience
- Not seeing results quickly enough
- Fear factors
- Being discouraged by others

All of these elements create obstacles to commitment, but the greatest of them is lack of clarity. In general, all others are ways people rationalize stopping their routines, which stems from losing clarity.

Understanding Urgent and Important Activities

Sometimes, it is not the obvious things that prevent you from achieving your goals or dreams—it is the very little and almost invisible things. When you are making shifts in your life, there are times when there is a blur between what is urgent and what is important. This blur can add to the lack of clarity, especially when you are in the middle of making a life shift.

You know how you walk into your restaurant sometimes and look around and there is chaos everywhere? How do you get the shift focused again? Like every great manager, you figure out what is going on, and you systematically start prioritizing what constitutes a "fire" and what can wait—what needs to be addressed immediately, and what can be addressed later. You immediately start making decisions about what is urgent, what is important, and what is unnecessary.

How do you know how to do this almost automatically? You have your *routine*; you have been trained to know what a good shift looks like and what a poor shift looks like, and you are clear on what the priorities of the restaurant are from shift to shift. Here is what is exciting: you learned how to do this in your restaurant and now you can learn how to do this in your life.

In Charles Hummel's 1967 book, *The Tyranny of the Urgent,* he asks, "Would a longer day really solve your problems?" His answer is a resounding **no**. The challenge, he asserts, is not that you do not have enough time. The real challenge is not being clear about your activities. Really consider your current activities for a moment and place them into two categories: "urgent" and "important." According to Hummel, "Your greatest danger is letting the urgent crowd out the important." How often has the day slipped away? After a busy day in the restaurant, how often have you realized that you have not completed any of your scheduled tasks? The reason for this time slipping away is the distinction between urgent and important.

Understanding Important

Important activities are tasks methodically moving you forward. Important tasks are time builders and require staying the course and staying focused on the tasks to achieve your goals even when they are met with resistance. Important activities in a restaurant include conducting orientations, completing inventories, insuring proper cash handling, training new team members, building community relations, completing scheduled maintenance checklists, or table touching during a busy shift.

However, in a busy, short-staffed and time-crunched shift, it is easy to blur urgent and important activities. Suddenly you are choosing urgent activities over training a new team member (or any of the other important activities that need to be addressed for the long-term viability of the restaurant). Sometimes, you might rationalize the urgent activities as being a necessity over the more important activities of investing in your business.

Understanding Urgent

Urgent priorities are the ones that you complete quickly and without much impact except for the immediate satisfaction of completing the task. E-mails and instant messaging are examples of urgent priorities. How often have you checked your e-mail and then replied to your entire inbox, only to realize that thirty or forty minutes had elapsed?

Urgent activities are time robbers and reactions to situations that result from not focusing on your important activities. Urgent priorities are sometimes referred to as spending the shift "putting out fires." Have you ever said something like, "I got absolutely nothing done because I spent the entire shift putting out fires?" Everybody, at some point in their careers, has said something similar; everyone has been a firefighter at some point too! Urgent activities give you a rush. You are in a perpetual state of activity, which makes you feel fantastic because you get consumed in doing things. The question is, however, "Does putting out fires actually help you move forward with what is really important in your life?"

The simplest definitions of urgent and important in relation to life shifts are listed below:

Important
- Important is the result of aligning your choices with your passions.
- Important is the forward progression toward your goals.
- Important is about managing your priorities with your time in order to create shifts of your life.
- Important is about investing your time today to build long-term success for the future.

Urgent
- Urgent is fire fighting.
- Urgent is a knee-jerk reaction.
- Urgent is a result of not managing your important priorities.
- Urgent can at times be a true crisis, like a hurricane.

The bottom line is that *urgent* activities are the time robbers of your shift; *important* activities are the time *builders* of your shifts.

Your Personal Clarity of Urgent and Important Activities

How do you support your *ROOTines* so you can stay focused on important activities? It begins by gaining your own personal clarity on the difference between urgent and important. Take a moment and calibrate your choices between urgent and important in your life.

Select which of the following are urgent activities, and which are important activities:

	Urgent	Important
➢ Returning every phone call immediately.	☐	☐
➢ Nonstop texting.	☐	☐
➢ Spending time surfing the Internet to see what's new, just in case you might need it.	☐	☐
➢ Having a meeting because you are required to have a meeting.	☐	☐
➢ Letting constant interruptions prevent you from getting something done.	☐	☐

➤ Spending time getting the   ☐   ☐
gossip on someone.

Managers sometimes view all of those choices as urgent because they believe that everything is a "fire." In fact, some managers can rationalize that everything is a necessity. Managers then start to postpone the important things or, even worse, they start addressing things that "will only take a few minutes." As a result, when everything is a priority then nothing is a priority. Think about your day: how much of your time is spent on addressing the urgent at the loss of investing in the important?

In the following list, choose the *urgent* and *important* activities:

	Urgent	Important
➤ Missing a friend's birthday party to attend a meeting.	☐	☐
➤ Rescheduling your vacation because a project deadline has been changed.	☐	☐
➤ Not exercising because you need more time to get more done at work.	☐	☐
➤ Running late because you have to squeeze that one last e-mail in before you can stop.	☐	☐
➤ Missing your child's school activity so you can prepare for the next month's meeting.	☐	☐
➤ Not checking in with loved ones because you don't have the time or energy to listen.	☐	☐

How often did you choose urgent over important? Is it really urgent, or is it a pattern of your life? I can remember one time a manager telling me that he missed the birth of his first child because he was investigating a cash-over-and-shortage at one of his restaurants. What important activities are you missing because your urgent activities are keeping you busy?

Try the exercise one more time, and imagine you have *six months to live*.

In the following list, choose the *urgent* and the *important* activities:

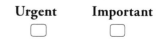

	Urgent	Important
➤ Missing a friend's birthday party to attend a meeting.	☐	☐

> Rescheduling your vacation because a
  project deadline has been changed.   ☐   ☐

> Not exercising because you need more
  time to get more done at work.   ☐   ☐

> Running late because you have to
  squeeze that one last e-mail in before
  you can stop.   ☐   ☐

> Missing your child's school activity so
  you can prepare for the next
  month's meeting.   ☐   ☐

> Not checking in with loved ones
  because you don't have the time or
  energy to listen.   ☐   ☐

Did your responses change? A key to a successful life is truly understanding what matters most to you as a person. It is your own definition, and it is one that will evolve and change over time. The key is to realize that life happens, and it is a good habit to recheck your definition and recalibrate your priorities, especially through the shifts of your life.

- Live your life with no regrets.
- Life is short, so don't wish, whine, or wait for it to happen.
- Embrace your challenges, and make them your opportunities.
- Extinguish the fears keeping you from moving your life forward.
- The greatest gifts we get in life sometimes come from our greatest losses.
- Anyone at any time can choose to live the best shifts of his or her life.

Your Head-and-Heart Connection

Understanding the connection between your head (your thoughts) and your heart (your feelings) can illuminate your important activities over your urgent activities. Linking the head to the heart creates a powerful connection, accelerating your ability to tell the difference between urgent and important. The following provides a closer look at the connection between your head and your heart.

Your Head

Your head and thoughts allow you to remain focused on the shifts of your life. Your head rationalizes the urgent over the important. The challenge lies in that your head can rationalize putting off important activities by constantly focusing on the thrill of urgent fires. Another way of looking at it is that we get a rush out of dealing with urgent fires and not so much of a rush dealing with everyday routines. However, managing everyday routines with a high level of efficiency and success can be a rush when you are achieving amazing shifts in your life.

Your Heart

The head doesn't always recognize the most important priorities in your life; it is looking for results and production. Sometimes it takes the heart to give you the stimulus to make a massive change. Your courage lies in your heart, allowing you to make important shifts to attain the best shifts of your life. "Courage" is rooted in the French word *coeur*, meaning "heart." The heart is your strongest muscle, fueled by passion and driven by your purpose. Your courage, passion and purpose give you the momentum to make important shifts in your life.

Your heart feels the difference between urgent and important. Your heart and feelings are the catalyst to develop the best shifts of your life. Your heart is an internal GPS system that instinctively wants good things for you and the people you care about. Your heart holds you true to your important activities, even if your head says differently.

Living solely driven by your heart or solely driven by your head prevents you from living your fullest life. Connecting your head and your heart can immediately align you to your goals and dreams. You feel confident, focused, and you stay connected to your important activities to positively move forward. You know your *ROOTines* are strong and right, so joy and empowerment fill you in each shift that you create.

Does Your Head-and-Heart Connection Happen Automatically?

Head-and-heart connections are not often automatic for everyone. Over time, with focus and intent, you can create an incredibly strong connection between your head and heart. Here are some suggestions to strengthen the connection between them:

- Invest in "the daily fifteen"—invest fifteen minutes each day to sit in complete silence. Slow your thoughts and breathing down, and try to listen to your heart. I do this every day, just to step back and reflect on things like:

1. What do I want to accomplish today?
2. How do I want to be a positive influence today?
3. What can I learn from yesterday that I can apply to today?
4. I review my *Life-Shift Plan* and *the Menu of Your Life.*
5. I just calm myself down to center in on having a great day!

- Keep a daily journal of your thoughts, experiences, and insights. Think about keeping a gratitude journal where you write down three things that you are grateful for as you begin or end your day. You will be amazed at how much more positive your life is when you begin the day from a position of gratitude.

- Focus your *ROOTine*—start each day with clear and focused activities about what you want to accomplish today. Write down your activities, and refer to them during the day. By focusing your intent, how much clearer are you about your important activities?

How will you know if your head-and-heart connection is strengthening? You will become much clearer about what is urgent and what is important. You will begin to gain greater clarity about your choices between urgent and important. You will find yourself making faster progress toward your goals and dreams. You will also be amazed at how strong and abundant your *ROOTine* becomes over the course of time!

Your Roots to Fruits

The journey of this book began with you seeing the realities of your life by shining light on them. Now you have the clarity and tools to make *ROOTines* to create consistent shifts in your life. This tree illustrates how all the steps of your journey come together to grow your tree with abundance.

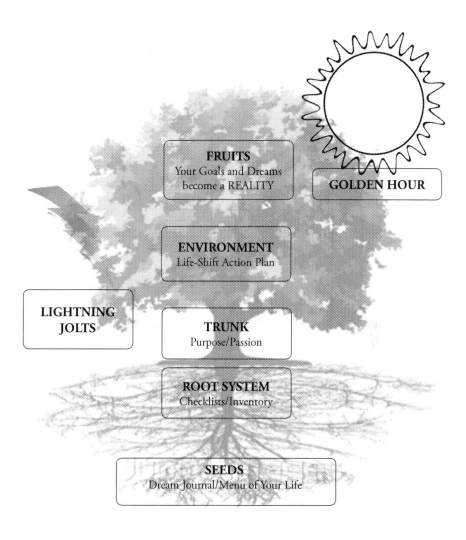

FRUITS
Your Goals and Dreams
become a REALITY

GOLDEN HOUR

ENVIRONMENT
Life-Shift Action Plan

LIGHTNING JOLTS

TRUNK
Purpose/Passion

ROOT SYSTEM
Checklists/Inventory

SEEDS
Dream Journal/Menu of Your Life

The Anatomy of Your Fruit Tree

SEEDS—All trees start with seeds. You have to choose what you are growing before you begin your planting. Your seeds are your dreams and goals from the *Menu of Your Life* and your *Dream List Journal*.

ROOT SYSTEMS—Once your seeds are planted, they begin to take root. The stronger the roots, the more solid and productive the tree becomes. Your goals and dreams are grounded in the strong root system of your *Love, Like, and Dislike Checklist; Timeframe Inventory, and* the important priorities of your life. All three grow stronger as you continue to stretch yourself to the new levels of clarity in both where you are and where you want to go.

TRUNK—The trunk of the tree is the most solid part and it grows from the inside out. Your purpose and passion are similar as they grow out from inside you, too. Your roots feed into your purpose, and your fruits benefit from the clarity of your purpose. The clearer your purpose, the stronger your trunk and roots will be and the more fruits you will produce. Your passion fuels your purpose to keep you strong, which also aids you in growing deep roots, resulting in the greatest abundance of fruits!

ENVIRONMENT—Healthy trees grow in healthy environments. Your Life-Shift Plan keeps you focused on your dreams and goals as life happens and shifts happen all around you in your day-to-day life. The healthier your environment, the more consistent results you will achieve.

LIGHTNING JOLTS—Trees face situations that can harm or jolt them into a new reality. Lightning is one of nature's reminders that you face obstacles and challenges in your growth. Some will come from within, and others will come from external sources. Equip your tree with a *FEAR Extinguisher*, and, when you are jolted with a new reality, you will be prepared to address it with Facts, E-motion, Action and Results.

Sometimes jolts may be wake-up calls. They may appear difficult at first, but they are meant to move you forward. For these types of jolts, you always have your personal board of directors supporting you as you are jolted into a new journey.

SUN—Everything in the universe grows with light. The sun represents the light that shines on your reality. The sun represents the *Golden Hour* that gives you that hour each day to reflect and re-ignite yourself to create the best shifts of your life. The more light you have, the clearer your choices are to achieve your goals and dreams!

Producing an Abundance of Fruit

Your *ROOTine* is the ongoing accomplishment of every step and activity in this book. You must germinate, sprout, and nurture each step to take the seeds of your dreams and goals, and grow them into the fruits of your reality.

1. Recognize that your daily *ROOTine* is tending to your seeds, your root system, and your entire tree to produce successful and fulfilling goals and dreams.

2. How do you know if your *ROOTines* are producing fruit?
    *   You feel happy.
    *   You feel passionate about your life.
    *   You are focused on important priorities.
    *   You are surrounded by positive people who support your dreams and goals.
    *   You treat others in the way they want to be treated.
    *   Your begin realizing your goals and dreams!

3. Your *ROOTines* may need some pruning if:
    *   You don't really feel excited or inspired about your life or your career.
    *   You no longer feel fueled by your passion.
    *   You feel jealous about another's accomplishments.
    *   You can't see the forest through the trees.
    *   You smile and claim to be happy externally; however, internally, you are miserable.

When the heart is right, the mind and body will follow.

—Coretta Scott King

Grow Your Own Roots to Fruits

Go back to your One Dream activity at the very beginning of the book. Use your One Dream and grow your own tree. Grow your own tree, fill in your tree and see the dreams become a reality.

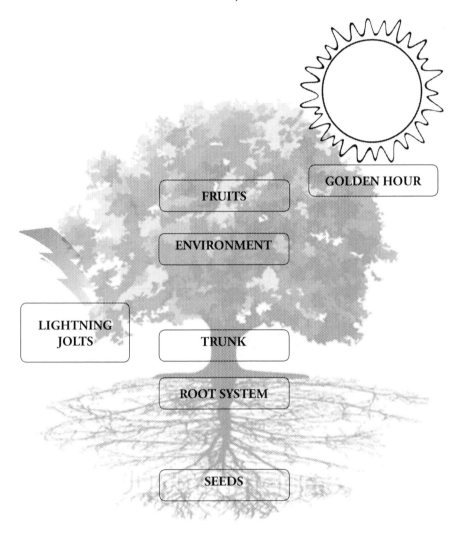

Closing Paperwork:
Giving Back Action Plan

Nearly every moment of every day we have the opportunity to give something to someone else—our time, our love, our resources. I have always found more joy in giving when I did not expect anything in return.

—Truett Cathy, Founder of Chick-fil-A

I don't think I have ever met a manager who loves closing paperwork! Closing paperwork typically happens very late at night after a long shift. It requires a great deal of administration, you typically cannot shortcut it, and you are required to complete it accurately before you can leave. I can remember many late nights with the closing crew and trying to reconcile a shortage in one of the tills while the crew waited.

Closing paperwork is a critical component to the success of your restaurant. The information in the closing paperwork is a "give back" to the next manager so they can make decisions on how they are going to set up the next day. It also gives back to management at corporate, so that they have real-time information to manage priorities based on the reported business realities. Closing paperwork has far-reaching implications for positively impacting your restaurant, even if it may not feel like that at two in the morning!

The idea of giving back, even through closing paperwork, is an important component for all successful managers. In today's competitive environment, successful restaurant managers are engaged in giving back to their communities. Experience has demonstrated time and time again that the more involved a restaurant manager is with their community, the more successful a restaurant will be in both good times and challenging times. This is such a powerful and important correlation that many companies have extensive and formal programs for Local Store Marketing and Community Relations activities.

There is an age-old adage that the more you give, the more you get. That speaks pretty clearly to the idea of giving back. Giving back is easy when you understand what you want to do and why. Here is a framework that I use to support managers as they gain their personal clarity on giving back. It consists of the following:

- What's your motivation for giving?
- Give your way.
- Give what you've got.
- Give thoughtfully.
- Start giving back today!

What's Your Motivation for Giving?

Most people want to make a difference, but they find it challenging to follow through with their good intentions. What prevents people from following through with good intentions? I would suggest that there are three primary reasons.

The first is fear—it can be overwhelming. Fear may underlie the following sentence: "I have worked hard for all that I have, and if I donate a portion of my earnings now, I may run out of money later." Or, "What if I give my time, my money, and my efforts and I still don't make a difference? I don't want my resources misspent."

The second is control. Control can be linked to the following sentence: "I feel great. Things are going my way, and I just don't want to do anything to stop this fantastic feeling." It is natural to clutch something so tightly that it prevents you from losing it. That tight-fisted clutch really comes from desiring control. Instead of holding tightly to what you have, try this: just let go. Here is something I always ask leaders to think about: the more you let go of control, the more control you get. The more you give, the more you get. What does that mean for you?

Finally, if an act of giving is not aligned with your passion, your purpose, your beliefs, and your values, it is difficult to feel committed to it. Listen to your heart.

Here are some thought starters to support you in deciding if you want to give back:

1. What would be the benefit of giving back to something that you believed in?
2. How could you personally benefit from giving back?
3. How could your career benefit from giving back?
4. What would be the benefit of giving back for your restaurant?

What is your motivation for giving back?

1. Do you want to make a difference in someone else's life?
2. Do you want to give to a group or organization that could benefit from your skill set?
3. Do you want to support an organization that represents something that you believe in?

It is essential that giving back-whether it is in the form of time or donation-serves the greater good of society. Sometimes understanding your motivation can be linked to your perspective. Here are two perspectives to take into consideration when thinking about giving back.

1. Thinking Abundantly
2. Aligning Your Passion and Your Purpose

Thinking Abundantly

When a fruit tree produces fruit, you have two choices: will you pick the fruit and help to grow more fruit, or will you let the fruit fall and rot? To prevent your fruit and your dreams from falling, you must create space for more fruit to grow. Think about your personal fruit tree. You can keep all of your fruit even if you are not using it all. Or you can share your fruit with the world, thereby enabling others to grow their own trees. Over time, one fruit tree could create an orchard.

Aligning Your Passion and Your Purpose

Enthusiasm is rooted in the meaning, "to be inspired." It is easy to give when you are inspired by your passion and your purpose. Living my life inspires me daily to share my gifts and fruits and give back in meaningful ways. I make it a priority to be involved in my community because I am grateful for the gifts that I have been given and want to share with others. I feel gratitude for my life when I am actively engaged in contributing to the "greater good."

Give Back Your Way

The act of giving back can be anything you want. As you begin to think about who or what you want to give back to, think about what is important to you. Where do you feel called to help? Are you good with children? Do you sympathize with the loneliness of some of the elderly? Is eliminating poverty or caring for the environment something that you feel passionate about?

Sometimes making the choice to give back can be as easy as making a toy donation to a local children's hospital, choosing to drop off groceries for someone in need, or spending time with an elderly neighbor. Every gesture, large or small, is appreciated when delivered from your heart.

Here is a great example of making a difference in a small way that resulted in a long-lasting impact. My dad loved to read. One of his favorite things to do was to read to all of his grandchildren. A highlight was every Christmas, when he would gather all of the grandkids around to read them one of his favorite Christmas stories.

He wanted to find a way to give back. He was living in a small town, and the local grade school was looking for ways to reengage the students in reading. My dad heard about this and worked with the school to set up a community–based reading day for the different classes. He was one of the first volunteers!

For years afterward, the school continued to use the reading program. Think about how many students' reading improved because of my dad's passion for reading to his grandchildren. One small step can lead to positively changing generations of people's lives.

Give What You've Got

Giving back meaningfully requires courage and confidence. Once you make the choice, it is simple because it is aligned with your life and your choices. Some ideas for giving back with your time, money, and ideas are listed below.

The following are ideas for sharing your time:
* Donate your time in your community.
* Spend time teaching a child to read.
* Spend time teaching an adult a skill to make him or her employable again.
* Spend time listening to a young adult without judgment or lecturing.

The following are ideas for sharing your financial resources:
- Clean out your closet or garage, and donate your belongings to others.
- Make a meal for a friend who is struggling.
- Give a can of food to the local food bank.
- Help someone get back on his or her feet again.

The following are examples for sharing your ideas:
- Share your business knowledge with a local nonprofit organization.
- Mentor a person who is trying to get to the next level in his or her career or a person in need.
- Volunteer or teach at a local school, business development service, or community-outreach program.
- Write articles to help others in their journeys.

Give Thoughtfully

The key to giving back meaningfully is quality, not quantity. It's easy to get caught up in that first moment of realizing you can help someone and make more promises than you can keep. If you are new to giving back, here are a few tips to support you in getting started.

- Do your homework and research organizations that interest you the most.
- Manage your enthusiasm and make sure not to over-commit.
- Cover your responsibilities and bow out respectfully if you have become involved in something that is not aligned with your goals or values.
- Start slowly, and grow your participation into the organization.
- Ask questions to ensure that your contribution is aligned with your passion and purpose.
- Ask friends to "shepherd" you into a cause or event that captures your interest.
- Keep your expectations realistic relative to your involvement so it's a win-win for everyone.

Start Giving Back Today!

The idea of giving back is equally important in the best shift of your life, too! A question frequently asked is, "Where do I start?" Start right here, right now. The more thoughtfully you choose to give, the more you live. By answering the following questions, you can create your own blueprint for giving.

1. Be clear about why you want to give back.
   List your reasons for why you want to give back.

2. What benefits will you realize by giving back?

3. Who do you want to share your fruits/gifts with?
   List the causes, people, or organizations that interest you.

4. What do you want to give?
   Evaluate your current priorities, and think of meaningful ways you can contribute.
   Remember, many organizations are looking for people who can just dedicate a couple of hours of time.

5. How will you give back?
   Research the two to three causes, people, or organizations that are important to you so that you can better understand ways that you can best be involved and be engaged.

6. Pick one of your two to three choices from above and write it below.

7. Write one action you can take in the next thirty minutes to start giving back.

8. Write one action you can take in the next twenty-four hours to give back.

9. Write one action you can take in the next week to give back.

10. Ultimately, how will you measure your success in effectively making a contribution?

Congratulations! You are well on your way to consistently creating amazing shifts in your life. By giving more, you choose to live more, and you ultimately create the best shifts in your life and in the lives of others!

We make a living by what we get; we make a life by what we give.

—Winston Churchill

The Next Shift:
Your Journey

o o o o o o o o o o o o o o o o o o o o o o o o o o o o o o o

I will act now. I will act now. I will act now. Henceforth, I will repeat these words each hour, each day, every day, until the words become as much a habit as my breathing and the action which follows becomes as instinctive as the blinking of my eyelids. With these words I can condition my mind to perform every action necessary for my success. I will act now. I will repeat these words again and again and again. I will walk where failures fear to walk. I will work when failures seek rest. I will act now for now is all I have. Tomorrow is the day reserved for the labor of the lazy. I am not lazy. Tomorrow is the day when the failure will succeed. I am not a failure. I will act now. Success will not wait. If I delay, success will become wed to another and lost to me forever. This is the time. This is the place. I am the person.

—Og Mandino

This last activity brings all of the activities in this book together into a master plan. It is specifically developed for you, by you. Your commitment to the completion of this book and the activities in it are to be congratulated and celebrated. You now have a system, tools and a process to continue to create the best shifts of your life.

While you are developing your plan, invest time and attention to be as clear as possible with your responses. If you have been completing the activities through the course of reading this book, you already have many of the responses completed. It is not just a matter of bringing everything together. As you begin to actualize your plan you will consistently achieve new levels of success and live a full and abundant life.

Planing Your Next Shift

1. Utilize your Golden Hour to choose one goal or dream from the *Menu of Your Life* or *Dream Journal*. Start with a goal or dream that is easily attainable and one that you feel passionate about in both your head and in your heart. Be as specific and detailed as possible in writing down your goal or dream.

2. Using your *Love, Like, and Dislike Checklist*, list everything you love about your life that supports your goal or dream. What adjustments do you need to make to your *Love, Like, and Dislike Checklist* to align your priorities?

3. Review your *Timeframes Inventory* activity. How will you manage your priorities to make your dream a reality? Identify your important activities, and stay focused on them; don't be distracted by urgent activities. Monitor your priorities to support and reinforce your dream. What choices can you make to develop habits to encourage your dreams and goals as they become your reality?

4. Leverage your purpose. Answer the following questions:
   How will your passion fuel you? What powerful values and beliefs inspire you and motivate you to succeed?

5. Complete a *Life-Shift Plan* to document and support your success in achieving your goal or your dream.

6. Extinguish any doubts or fears you have by using the *FEAR Extinguisher* as part of your process. Review your responses. What new choices can you make right now to move your fear to a positive reality?

7. Check your *ROOTine*. Are you committed to growing your dream each day? Is your dream growing or rotting? What choices can you make right now to grow a strong tree?

8. Remember: on your journey for continued success, it is important to always give back! The more you give, the more you get. So try to incorporate your give-back actions into your plan.

9. Measure your success:
   • How are you doing? Are you energized?
   • Are you making the progress you want, according to the *Life-Shift Plan* Timeline?
   • Are you facing any time robbers or roadblocks to realizing your goals and dreams?
   • What adjustments do you need to make to realize your goals and dreams?
   • Are you using your personal board of directors to stay on course?
   • Do you need to make any other new choices to accelerate your goals or dreams?

10. Celebrate your success. Realize your goal or dream. You have now experienced the power of living the life of your goals and dreams!

Most importantly, **don't stop!** When you realize one dream or goal, select another one to achieve. The more you practice, the easier and faster you will achieve more dreams and goals. I have used everything in this book multiple times to support the shifts of my life. You now have the knowledge, power, and experience to utilize this same system to support *you* in the shifts of *your* life.

Continue to utilize everything you have done and apply it to another goal or dream. If you choose to continue, realizing your dreams will become one of your greatest *ROOTines*. Enjoy your goals and dreams, and look forward to achieving a lifetime of them!

The Best Shift: Moving Forward!

In his 2005 book, *The Tao of Leadership*, John Heider writes about the "ripple effect," explaining that one's behavior influences others through the ripple effect. According to the ripple effect, your shifts could have potentially infinite consequences. Your shifts influence your family and friends. Their shifts influence your community; the community's shifts influence your nation; and the nation's shifts influence your world. It all begins with your shift!

My goal and dream is that you create the best shifts of your life and create a powerful ripple effect to shift the world. Thank you for this journey, and enjoy The BEST Shift of Your Life!
—Kathleen Wood, Author and Founder, Kathleen Wood Partners, LLC

About the Author

Kathleen Wood is the founder of Kathleen Wood Partners, an innovative strategy firm specializing in shifting leaders and businesses to new levels of success. Kathleen Wood Partners consults with clients to clarify and align their purposes to accelerate their growth and profitability. She holds a bachelor of science degree in hotel and restaurant management from the University of Wisconsin-Stout and an MBA from Loyola University of Chicago. For more information about Kathleen Wood Partners, visit www.kwoodpartners.com.